I0427796

Integrated Safety Analysis Guidance Document

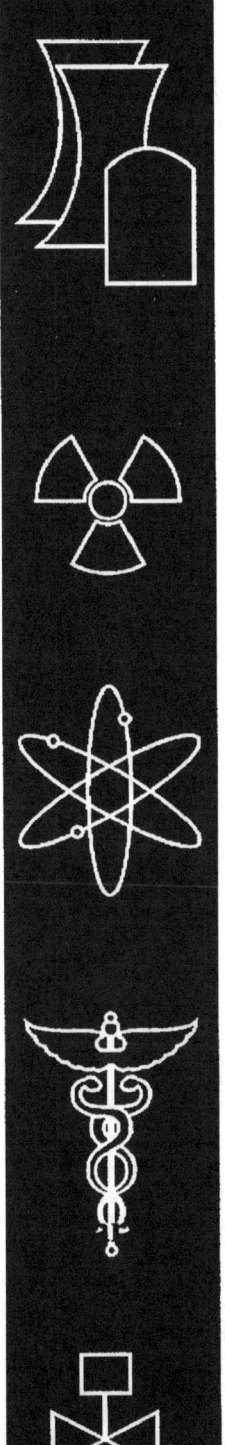

U. S. Nuclear Regulatory Commission
Office of Nuclear Material Safety and Safeguards
Washington, DC 20555-0001

AVAILABILITY OF REFERENCE MATERIALS
IN NRC PUBLICATIONS

NUREG-1513

Integrated Safety Analysis
Guidance Document

Date Completed: May 2001
Date Published: May 2001

Prepared by
R.. I. Milstein

Division of Fuel Cycle Safety and Safeguards
Office of Nuclear Material Safety and Safeguards
U.S. Nuclear Regulatory Commission
Washington, DC 20555-0001

ABSTRACT

On September 18, 2000, the U. S. Nuclear Regulatory Commission published a final rule, 10 CFR Part 70, for licensing the use of special nuclear material. In this rule, NRC included a requirement that certain licensee/applicants subject to 10 CFR 70 conduct an integrated safety analysis (ISA). The purpose of this document is to provide general guidance to NRC fuel cycle licensee/applicants on how to perform an integrated safety analysis (ISA) and document the results. In particular, the document defines an ISA, identifies its role in a facility's safety program, identifies and describes several generally accepted ISA methods, and provides guidance in choosing a method.

The approaches and methods described in this document are not a substitute for NRC regulations, and compliance is not required. This document does not itself impose regulatory requirements, nor does it address acceptance criteria for an ISA. As discussed in Section 1.3, "Purpose of Document," acceptance criteria for ISA are addressed in the "Standard Review Plan for the Review of a License Application for a Fuel Cycle Facility," draft NUREG-1520.

CONTENTS

LIST OF FIGURES

LIST OF TABLES

1 INTRODUCTION

1.1 Historical Context

An integrated safety analysis (ISA) is a systematic examination of a facility's processes, equipment, structures, and personnel activities to ensure that all relevant hazards that could result in unacceptable consequences have been adequately evaluated and appropriate protective measures have been identified.

Although the application of formal ISA techniques (known in the chemical industry as process hazard analysis (PHA)) was established about 40 years ago, its growth in recent years was spurred by a number of serious chemical accidents that illustrated the need to ensure a higher level of safety. In analyzing the causes of these accidents and the response of management, it was recognized that the correction of problems after an accident occurs is not necessarily conducive to the prevention of future accidents. Although the immediate problem may be solved, a systematic analysis of the entire facility is needed to identify other, unrelated potential accidents, and the measures needed to prevent their occurrence or mitigate their consequences.

The recognition of ISA as a critical element in managing process safety is evidenced in the industry standards that have been developed (American Institute of Chemical Engineers (1992)[1], American Petroleum Institute (1990), and Chemical Manufacturing Association (1992)) as well as recent State (New Jersey (1986), California (1986), Delaware (1988), and Nevada (1991)) and Federal regulations (Occupational Safety and Health Administration (OSHA) (1996), U.S. Environmental Protection Agency (EPA) (1994), and U.S. Department of Energy (DOE) orders (1994)).

1.2 Regulatory Basis

On September 18, 2000, the U.S. Nuclear Regulatory Commission published a final rule, 10 CFR Part 70, for licensing the use of special nuclear material. In this rule, NRC included a requirement that certain licensees/applicants subject to 10 CFR Part 70 conduct an ISA. The ISA is expected to form the basis of a safety program that requires adequate controls and systems to be in place to ensure the safe operation of the facility. Recognizing that NRC fuel cycle facilities are, to a large extent, chemical processing plants, the ISA techniques that have been applied to plants in the chemical and petrochemical industries are generally applicable to the NRC facilities. In fact, their application at other (non-NRC) nuclear fuel cycle facilities is well established. Nuclear fuel reprocessing plants (e.g., Idaho Chemical Processing Plant (ICPP) and Barnwell) developed and applied ISA methods in the 1970s; other DOE fuel cycle facilities developed and applied ISAs in the 1980s. ISA techniques applied to nuclear fuel cycle facilities must address the special hazards that are present at such facilities and their potential for causing criticality

---

[1]References are cited herein by author and date of publication.

incidents and radiological releases, as well as certain chemical releases.

1.3 Purpose of Document

The purpose of this document is to provide guidance to NRC fuel cycle licensees/applicants on how to perform an ISA and document the results. In particular, this document emphasizes several generally accepted approaches that are used to identify the hazards and accident sequences that occur in chemical processing plants. It does not emphasize or describe specific methods for evaluating the likelihood of accidents, nor estimating their consequences. There are other critical elements that make up a robust safety program, such as training, maintenance, incident investigation, emergency planning, etc.; this document discusses these elements only as they are affected by the ISA process. It does not provide detailed guidance about these elements. Nor does it address acceptance criteria for the ISA. Instead, these topics are addressed in the "Standard Review Plan for the Review of a License Application for a Fuel Cycle Facility," draft NUREG-1520. In particular, likelihood evaluation methods are described in Appendix A to the ISA chapter of this Standard Review Plan. Appropriate ISA consequence evaluation methods are described in NUREG/CR-6410, Nuclear Fuel Cycle Facility Accident Analysis Handbook.

In developing the ISA guidance for its licensees, NRC has relied on information from various sources, with particular emphasis on information in Guidelines for Hazard Evaluation Procedures, Second Edition With Worked Examples, developed by the American Institute of Chemical Engineers (1992). This reference book contains descriptions of most ISA techniques currently in use. Examples of the application of ISA methods to nuclear fuel cycle facilities, which are found in Appendix B, were provided under contract to NRC by Savannah River Technology Center.

NRC is also cognizant of regulations on Process Safety Management of Highly Hazardous Chemicals, developed by OSHA (1996) and Risk Management Programs for Chemical Accidental Release Prevention, developed by EPA (1994). The ISA guidance provided in this document is intended to be consistent with the requirements of OSHA and EPA so as to minimize the regulatory burden on NRC licensees. It should be recognized, however, that the scope of NRC's concerns differs from those of OSHA and EPA. NRC is responsible for addressing radiological, nuclear criticality, and certain chemical hazards (i.e. UF_6 release) not covered under other regulations. Therefore, while it is anticipated that analyses done to satisfy requirements of OSHA and EPA may be useful, it is also expected that such analyses will need to be extended to address NRC requirements.

The information collections contained in this NUREG are covered by the requirements of 10 CFR Part 70, which were approved by the Office of Management and Budget, approval number 3150-0009.

Public Protection Notification

If a means used to impose an information collection does not display a currently valid OMB control number, the NRC may not conduct or sponsor, and a person is not required to respond to, the information collection.

1.4 Outline of This Document

The document will discuss the following:

- Definition of an ISA

- The role of ISA in a facility's safety program

- ISA methods

- Choosing an ISA method

- Choosing an ISA team

- Conducting the ISA

- Documenting the results

2 INTEGRATED SAFETY ANALYSIS

2.1 Definition

According to the revised Part 70, an integrated safety analysis means

> "a systematic analysis to identify facility and external hazards and their potential for initiating accident sequences, the potential accident sequences, their likelihood and consequences, and the items relied on for safety. As used here, *integrated* means joint consideration of, and protection from, all relevant hazards, including radiological, nuclear criticality, fire, and chemical."

In essence, ISA is a systematic examination of a facility's processes, equipment, structures, and personnel activities to ensure that all relevant hazards that could result in unacceptable consequences have been adequately evaluated and appropriate protective measures have been identified. In general, the ISA should provide:

- a description of the structures, equipment, and process activities at the facility,

- an identification and systematic analysis of hazards at the facility,

- a comprehensive identification of potential accident/event sequences that would result in unacceptable consequences, and the expected likelihoods of those sequences,

- an identification and description of controls (i.e., structures, systems, equipment, or components) that are relied on to limit or prevent potential accidents or mitigate their consequences, and

- an identification of measures taken to ensure the availability and reliability of identified safety systems.

At NRC-licensed fuel cycle facilities, the unacceptable consequences of concern (within NRC's regulatory authority) include those that result in the exposure of workers or members of the public to excessive levels of radiation and hazardous concentrations of certain chemicals. The mechanism for such exposure could be a release of radioactive material, or an inadvertent nuclear chain reaction involving special nuclear material (criticality). The release of hazardous chemicals is also of regulatory concern to NRC but only to the extent that such hazardous releases result from the processing of licensed nuclear material or have the potential for adversely affecting radiological safety. OSHA and EPA are responsible for regulating all other aspects of chemical safety at the facility.

There are a number of ISA hazard evaluation methods that may be used to analyze the process hazards at NRC-licensed facilities (see Section 2.3, "ISA Hazard Evaluation Methods"). Although these techniques were established primarily as tools to analyze process hazards at chemical facilities (i.e., explosive and toxic materials), they can be logically extended to address radiological and nuclear criticality hazards.

In general, ISA techniques use either an inductive or a deductive analysis approach. The inductive (or bottom-up) approach attempts to identify possible accident sequences by examining, in detail, deviations from normal operating conditions. Except for the event tree method, most inductive methods are best suited for analyzing single-failure events (i.e., those events caused by the failure of a single control). (With some effort, some of the inductive methods may be extended to address multi-failure events.) The deductive (or "top-down") approach, on the other hand, is more suited for identifying combinations of equipment failures and human errors that can result in an accident (i.e., multi-failure events). Usually, the deductive approach identifies a top event (usually a severe consequence), and attempts to explain the various ways (including single- and multi-failure events) that the top event can occur. Generally, the inductive approaches are useful in identifying a broad range of potential accidents. The deductive approaches, on the other hand, provide a deeper understanding of the mechanism by which a particular accident might occur. That is, they help identify the possible pathways (i.e., combinations of failures) and root causes that could lead to an accident. By identifying the root causes, the deductive approaches can provide assurance that common-mode failures are understood and are properly addressed.

One potentially effective approach for implementing an ISA program is to combine the two types of techniques, using the inductive approach (e.g., HAZOP) to identify the broad range of potential accidents and the deductive approach (qualitative Fault-Tree) to analyze in detail the most significant of those accidents (or any others that are postulated). For example, suppose that a HAZOP analysis identified a potential explosion that could result in a significant radiological release and exposure of the public. A fault-tree analysis might then be used to identify the other combinations of failures which could cause the explosion and the controls used to prevent or mitigate the accident to acceptable levels of risk.

2.2 The Role of ISA In a Facility's Safety Program

One of the results of an ISA is the identification of controls, both engineered and administrative, that are needed to limit or prevent accidents or mitigate their effects. The identification of controls, however, is not sufficient to guarantee an adequate level of safety. In addition, an effective management system is needed to ensure that, when called on, these controls are in place and are operating properly. Elements to be addressed in the management system include:

1. Procedures (development, review, approval, and implementation)
2. Training and Qualification
3. Maintenance, Calibration, and Surveillance
4. Management of Change (Configuration Management)
5. Quality Assurance
6. Audits and Self-Assessments
7. Incident Investigation
8. Records Management

The importance of these management elements cannot be overstated. ISA may be capable of identifying potential accidents and the controls needed to prevent them, but it cannot ensure effective implementation of the controls and their proper operation. Without a strong management control system in place, the safety of a facility cannot be ensured.

2.3 ISA Hazard Evaluation Methods

The American Institute of Chemical Engineers (AIChE) (1992) provides information on the most common hazard evaluation techniques used for analyzing process systems and identifying potential accidents.[2] Chapter 4 of that reference provides an overview of each technique including a short description, the purpose of using the technique, the types of results obtained, and the resource requirements. Chapter 6 provides a more comprehensive discussion including information on the technical approach, analysis procedure, anticipated work product, and available computer aids. In addition, each method is illustrated with a brief example. Finally, Part II of AIChE (1992) "Worked Examples," provides practical, detailed examples of how some of the ISA methods are applied.

To demonstrate the application of the ISA methods to facilities that process nuclear materials, Appendix B of this guidance document provides several examples of the application of these methods to processes taken from the nuclear fuel cycle.

Twelve methods are discussed in AIChE (1992):

----

[2]There are other references that describe ISA methodologies. However, the AIChE text is clear, comprehensive, and is well-suited to practitioners of hazard analysis.

1. Safety Review
2. Checklist Analysis
3. Relative Ranking
4. Preliminary Hazard Analysis
5. What-If Analysis
6. What-If/Checklist Analysis
7. Hazard and Operability Analysis (HAZOP)
8. Failure Modes and Effects Analysis (FMEA)
9. Fault Tree Analysis
10. Event Tree Analysis
11. Cause-Consequence Analysis
12. Human Reliability Analysis

The first five methods (Safety Review, Checklist Analysis, Relative Ranking, Preliminary Hazard Analysis, and What-If Analysis) are considered to be particularly useful when a broad identification and overview of hazards is required (see Section 2.6.1, "Scope of Analysis"). The next three methods (What-If/Checklist, HAZOP, and FMEA) are more suitable for performing detailed analyses of a wide range of hazards, to identify potential accident sequences. The last four methods (Fault Tree, Event Tree, Cause-Consequence Analysis, Human Reliability Analysis) are best used to provide in-depth analysis of specific accidents that have been identified using other methods. In general, their use requires a higher degree of analyst expertise and increased time and effort.

The methods identified in this section are all considered "qualitative" methods in the sense that they can provide important insights useful for reducing risk without requiring a quantitative estimation of risk. Some of the qualitative methods (e.g., HAZOP, FMEA, Fault Tree, and Event Tree) may also be used to provide input to a full quantitative risk assessment (QRA). QRA, which is most often used when the consequences of an accident are very severe, is a technique that provides quantitative estimates of the risk of accidents. In addition to providing information useful for prioritizing measures for reducing risk, QRA can also be used to demonstrate that the frequency of occurrence of a severe accident is acceptably small. Guidance for licensees interested in conducting a QRA is provided in AIChE (1989).

In addition to the methods identified above, several other approaches have been developed in industries other than the chemical process industry. These include the Hazard Barrier Target technique, Digraph Analysis, Management Oversight Risk Tree (MORT) Analysis, Hazard Warning Structure, and Multiple Failure/Error Analysis. The MORT approach is particularly useful in analyzing the role of management and management systems in preventing accidents and would be a useful supplement to other techniques (Johnson, 1973; Johnson, 1980; Knox and Eicher, 1983).

Both EPA's proposed Risk Management Program rule (40 CFR Part 68) and OSHA's Process Safety Management Rule (29 CFR 1910.119) require the use of one or more of the following

ISA approaches:

What-If, Checklist, What-If/Checklist, HAZOP, FMEA, Fault Tree Analysis, or an appropriate equivalent method.

2.4 Choosing An ISA Hazard Evaluation Method

The choice of a particular method or combination of methods will depend on a number of factors including the reason for conducting the analysis, the results needed from the analysis, the information available, the complexity of the process being analyzed, the personnel and experience available to conduct the analysis, and the perceived risk of the process. Based on these factors, Appendix A (AIChE, 1992) provides a detailed flow chart that guides the ISA practitioner in choosing a particular method. If an approach has been chosen to satisfy OSHA and EPA regulations, and if its use is appropriate for addressing NRC concerns, consideration may be given to using that method for conducting an ISA.

One of the most important factors in determining the choice of an ISA approach is the information that is needed from the analysis. To satisfy NRC requirements as defined in Part 70, the licensee/applicant should choose a method capable of identifying specific accident/event sequences in addition to the safety controls that prevent such accidents or mitigate their consequences. Each of the methods discussed below have this capability.

For identifying single-failure events (i.e., those accidents that result from the failure of a single control), What-If, Preliminary Hazard Analysis, What-If/Checklist, FMEA, or HAZOP are the recommended approaches. Appendix B.1 provides, as an example, partial results from a What-If analysis of criticality hazards present during the pelletizing, rod loading, and fuel bundle assembly operations at a fuel fabrication facility. Because criticality events are perceived to be high risk, redundant controls are normally provided to preclude their occurrence. Although the What-If technique is not the optimum choice for analyzing redundant systems, useful results were obtained, in this case, by considering separately the failures of the moderation and geometry control systems. To explicitly demonstrate adherence to the double contingency principle, however, the What-If analysis should be supplemented by the application of an approach more suited to redundant systems, such as the qualitative fault tree method.

According to AIChE (1992), the choices identified above (i.e., What-If, Preliminary Hazard Analysis, What-If/Checklist, FMEA, or HAZOP) should be narrowed to the latter three approaches if the perceived risk of the potential accident sequences is high. At a nuclear fuel fabrication facility, one of the most safety-significant operations is the vaporization of uranium hexafluoride$_6$ (UF_6). Because of the potential occurrence of an inadvertent criticality or the release of toxic UF_6 and hydrogen fluoride (HF), the vaporization process is a good candidate for analysis by the HAZOP method, a structured technique that is particularly suited for analysis of chemical operations. Appendix B.2 contains excerpts of results obtained from a HAZOP analysis of a UF_6 dry conversion process.

8

If the results of the ISA are expected to be used as input into a QRA study, then HAZOP, FMEA, Fault-Tree, Event-Tree, or Human Reliability Analysis are the approaches recommended by AIChE (1992). Even if a QRA study is not envisioned, these methods (as well as Cause-Consequence Analysis) are recommended if the accidents analyzed are likely to result in consequences caused by multiple failures.[3] At a nuclear fuel fabrication plant, because of the potentially serious consequences resulting from a release of UF_6 during vaporization, a qualitative fault tree analysis of this event is justified, particularly to identify the redundant systems that are available to provide protection. Appendix B.3 contains the results of a fault tree analysis used to model the sequences of events that could lead to a release of UF_6.

Some ISA methods are more systematic than others. For example, the HAZOP technique provides a detailed framework for studying each process, line by line, in an exhaustive manner. Each process variable (such as flow, temperature, pressure), a description of deviations from normal values, potential consequences of these deviations, and existing controls, are recorded. Another systematic approach, FMEA, considers the various failure modes of equipment items and evaluates the effects of these failures on the system or plant. On the other hand, the What-If technique relies on a relatively unstructured "brainstorming" approach to create a list of questions addressing hazards or specific accident events that could produce an undesirable consequence in a system or process. Whereas the structured nature of the HAZOP and FMEA approaches may partially compensate for weaknesses in the analysis team, the What-if technique, to a greater extent, relies on the experience and knowledge of the hazard analysis team for its thoroughness and success.

For ISAs performed to comply with the revised 10 CFR Part 70, the analysis must specifically identify the items relied on for safety (IROFS). In addition, the ISA must evaluate whether the system of IROFS in place in a process will make the identified accidents sufficiently unlikely to meet the likelihood requirements of section 70.61. To accomplish this evaluation, the ISA must show each sequence of failures of IROFS that leads to the consequences of concern to section 70.61. Thus, the results of the evaluation must include a diagram, tabulation, or descriptive list that describes each accident as a sequence of IROFS failures or natural phenomena events, and that identifies the consequences of that sequence. For accident sequences involving multiple events, some of the hazard evaluation techniques identified above do not produce output in this form. For these methods, such as HAZOP and What If-Checklist, the tabulation or diagraming of accident sequences is an additional step. Fault Trees and Event Trees, which are the recommended methods for multiple failure scenarios, do provide an implicit display of the accident sequences and IROFS. The ISA required under 10 CFR Part 70 also requires that a separate descriptive list of items relied on for safety (IROFS) be prepared. These requirements are explained fully in the ISA chapter of the standard review plan for Part 70.

In addition to the ISA hazard evaluation methods described above, there are additional methods

---

[3]HAZOP and FMEA, although primarily used to address single-failure events, can be extended to address multiple failure situations.

or tools, also considered part of the ISA approach, that are used to identify hazards at the facility and to analyze the consequences of potential accidents. For identifying hazards at the facility and their potential interactions, the interaction matrix approach identified in Section 2.6.3 of this document should be considered. For analyzing the consequences of potential accidents, the methods identified in the "Nuclear Fuel Cycle Facility Accident Analysis Handbook," (NUREG/CR-6410,U.S. Nuclear Regulatory Commission, 1998) should be considered.

2.5 Choosing A Team

One of the most important factors in ensuring a successful ISA is the knowledge and experience of the team that is assembled to perform the analysis. Although each method may present a somewhat different rationale for choosing team members, there are some general principles that should be followed. First, the leader of the team should be knowledgeable in the chosen ISA method. This would imply that the leader have formal training in that particular method. The leader should have a thorough understanding of process operations and hazards, but, to avoid a conflict of interest, he should not be the designated expert (e.g., the process engineer) on the process being analyzed. Also, the leader should be able to interact effectively with a diverse group, to build a team consensus. Second, at least one member of the team should have specific and detailed experience in the process being analyzed. Third, the team should consist of members who have a variety of expertise and experience. In particular, engineering, maintenance, and process operations experience should be represented. The presence of process operators is especially important since they have a practical understanding of how the process operates and how problems are likely to occur. Specific safety disciplines such as radiological, criticality, and chemical should also be represented when these hazards are important. In addition, an individual needs to be assigned the responsibility of recording the proceedings in a systematic fashion.

The composition of the team is somewhat dependent on the method used. An approach that is highly systematic like the HAZOP and FMEA analyses may not require the same degree of expertise as a less systematic approach such as the "What-If," which relies to a greater extent on the experience of the team members.

2.6 Conducting The ISA

2.6.1 Scope of Analysis

2.6.1.1 Consequences of Concern
Before conducting the ISA, it is important to define the scope of the analysis including the consequences of concern. In general, NRC is interested in radiological, nuclear criticality, and certain chemical consequences that can affect worker or public safety. In particular, section 70.61 of NRC's revision to Part 70 defines two categories of consequences of concern to the ISA, high consequence and intermediate consequence events. High consequence events are

defined in terms of specific exposure levels or health effects to workers and persons off-site. In particular, they include any acute chemical exposure to an individual from licensed material or hazardous chemicals produced from licensed material that:

  (i) Could endanger the life of a worker, or
  (ii) Could lead to irreversible or other serious, long-lasting health effects to any individual located outside the controlled area.

Intermediate consequence events are defined by similar, but lower, exposure levels. The approach for an ISA addressing 10 CFR 70.61 should be designed specifically to identify those accidents capable of producing these consequences. This can be facilitated by performance of scoping consequence analyses early during the ISA, and surveying the locations of processes and hazards capable of producing them. These analyses can be used to screen out situations or processes not capable of the consequences of concern, and to assure that all processes that are capable of producing them are analyzed.

To ensure an acceptable level of risk at a facility, 10 CFR 70.61 requires that sufficient controls be in place so that the occurrence of any credible high consequence event is "highly unlikely," and the occurrence of any credible intermediate consequence event is "unlikely." Definitions for these likelihood terms are provided in "Standard Review Plan for the Review of a License Application for a Fuel Cycle Facility," draft NUREG-1520.

2.6.1.2 Physical Scope of Analysis

The ISA should take into account the following factors in conducting the analysis: site characteristics, the structures on the site, the equipment and materials in use, the processes in operation, and the personnel operating the facility. Credible external events resulting from meteorological and seismological phenomena and their potential for causing accidents at the facility also need to be addressed. Meteorological phenomena would include tornados, hurricanes, precipitation, and flooding.

2.6.1.3 Analysis Assumptions

Any assumptions made in performing the ISA should be explicitly documented and examined for reasonableness. For example, any initiating events deemed to be "incredible," such as airplane crashes, meteorite impact, etc., should be justified and documented. By documenting the assumptions, the licensee will be better able to recognize any future changes that invalidate the assumptions and thus require modification to the ISA.

2.6.2 Process Safety Information

Detailed and accurate information about plant processes is essential for conducting a complete and thorough ISA. In fact, the absence of certain types of process safety information may prevent the use of a particular ISA method or may delay the performance of an ISA.

The type of information available to perform an ISA varies depending on the life cycle of the process or facility being analyzed. During the early stages of the life cycle (i.e., research and development, conceptual design), only basic chemical and physical data may be available. At the detailed design stage, additional information specific to the process may be compiled. Finally, during the operations stage, a wealth of new information, based on operating history, is expected to become available. Since the value of the ISA is directly related to the completeness and accuracy of the process safety information that is available for use, the analysis of an operating facility may provide more meaningful results than a similar analysis of a new facility or process.

Tables 2.1 and 2.2 (AIChE, 1992) provide a comprehensive list of process safety information that may be needed to perform an ISA. In addition, OSHA (1996) has identified a minimum set of process safety information that it believes is necessary to conduct process hazard analyses for those areas/materials under OSHA purview. The information is categorized as pertaining to hazardous chemicals, to the technology of the process, and to the equipment in the process.

Table 2.1 Examples of Information Used to Perform a Hazard Evaluation Study

- Chemical reaction equations and stoichiometry for primary and important secondary or side reactions
- Type and nature of catalysts used
- Reactive chemical data on all streams, including in-process chemicals
- Kinetic data for important process reactions, including the order, rate constants, approach to equilibrium, etc.
- Kinetic data for undesirable reactions, such as decompositions and autopolymerizations
- Process limits stated in terms of pressure, temperature, concentration, feed-to-catalyst ratio, etc., along with a description of the consequences of operating beyond these limits
- Process flow diagrams and a description of the process steps or unit operations involved, starting with raw material storage and feed preparation and ending with product recovery and storage
- Design energy and mass balances
- Major material inventories
- Description of general control philosophy (i.e., identifying the primary control variables and the reasons for their selection)
- Discussion of special design considerations that are required because of the unique hazards or properties of the chemicals involved
- Safety, health, and environmental data for raw materials, intermediates, products, by-products, and wastes
- Regulatory limits and/or permit limits
- Applicable codes and standards
- Variances
- Plot plans

- Area electrical classification drawings
- Building and equipment layouts
- Electrical classifications of equipment
- Piping and instrumentation drawings
- Mechanical equipment data sheets
- Equipment catalogs
- Vendor drawings and operation and maintenance manuals
- Valve and instrumentation data sheets
- Piping specifications
- Utility specifications
- Test and inspection reports
- Electrical one-line drawings
- Instrument loop drawings and logic diagrams
- Control system and alarm description
- Computer control system hardware and software design
- Operating procedures (with critical operating parameters)
- Maintenance procedures
- Emergency response plan and procedures
- Relief system design basis
- Ventilation system design basis
- Safety system(s) design basis
- Fire protection system(s) design basis
- Incident reports
- Meteorological data
- Population distribution data
- Site hydrology data
- Previous safety studies
- Internal standards and checklists
- Corporate safety Policies
- Relevant industry experience

Table 2.2 Common Material Property Data for Hazard Identification

Acute toxicity
- inhalation (e.g, LC_{LO})
- oral (e.g., LD_{50})
- dermal

Chronic toxicity
- inhalation
- oral
- dermal

Carcinogenicity

Mutagenicity

Teratogenicity

Exposure limits
- TLV
- PEL
- STEL
- IDLH
- ERPG

Biodegradability

Aquatic toxicity

Persistence in the environment

Odor threshold

Physical properties
- freezing point
- coefficient of expansion
- boiling point
- solubility

Physical properties (cont'd)
- vapor pressure
- density or specific volume
- corrosivity/erosivity
- heat capacity
- specific heats

Reactivity
- process materials
- desired reaction(s)
- side reaction(s)
- decomposition reaction(s)
- kinetics
- materials of construction
- raw material impurities
- contaminants (air, water, rust, lubricants, etc.)
- decomposition products
- incompatible chemicals
- pyrophoric materials

Stability
- shock
- temperature
- light
- polymerization

Flammability/Explosivity
- LEL/LFL
- UEL/UFL
- dust explosion parameters
- minimum ignition energy
- flash point
- autoignition temperature
- energy production

Abbreviations:

ERPG	Emergency Response Planning Guidelines	STEL	Short Term Exposure Limit
IDLH	Immediately Dangerous to Life and Health	TLV	Threshold Limit Value
LEL	Lower Explosive Limit	UEL	Upper Explosive Limit
LFL	Lower Flammable Limit	UFL	Upper Flammable Limit
PEL	Permissible Exposure Level		

Regarding hazardous chemicals, OSHA requires (29 CFR 1910.119) compilation of the following information: toxicity information, permissible exposure limits, physical data, reactivity data, corrosivity data, thermal and chemical stability data, and hazardous effects of inadvertent mixing of different chemicals. Information about specific materials can be obtained from the chemical suppliers and manufacturers who can provide material safety data sheets (MSDSs), product literature, and general chemical expertise. Information can also be obtained from industrial and professional organizations such as the AIChE, the American Petroleum Institute (API), or the Chemical Manufacturers Association (CMA).

For the technology of the process, OSHA requires assembling the following information: a block flow diagram or simplified process flow diagram, process chemistry, maximum intended inventory, safe upper and lower limits for such items as temperatures, pressures, flows, and compositions.

Regarding the equipment used in the process, OSHA requires collecting the following information: materials of construction, piping and instrumentation diagrams (P&IDs), electrical classification, relief system design and design basis, ventilation system design, design codes and standards employed, material and energy balances, and safety systems (e.g., interlocks, detection, and suppression systems).

A minimum set of process safety information considered acceptable for performing an ISA is addressed in "Standard Review Plan for the Review of a License Application for a Fuel Cycle Facility," draft NUREG-1520.

For the results of the ISA to be valid, the information required to perform the ISA must be accurate and current. If such information is not available, then the information must be developed to permit the performance of an ISA.

2.6.3 Hazard Identification

A hazard is defined as an inherent physical, radiological, or chemical characteristic that has the potential for causing harm to people, to the environment or to property. Before an analysis of hazards can begin, it is first necessary to identify those hazards. Although NRC's primary responsibility is to regulate radiological hazards, the Agency also addresses certain hazardous chemicals (i.e., those chemicals that are radioactive themselves, that result from the processing of licensed nuclear material, or that have the potential for adversely affecting radiological safety).

To identify hazards at a facility, certain types of information should be available regarding the materials used at the facility. For uranium and other materials that pose radiological hazards, the radiological properties of concern should be identified (e.g., radioactive half-life, biological half-life, decay mode, etc.). In addition, the conditions under which available fissionable material could support a self-sustaining nuclear reaction (i.e., pose a criticality hazard) should be identified. For addressing chemical hazards, typical material properties such as toxicity,

15

flammability, reactivity, etc. should be considered by the licensee (see Table 2.2 of this document and OSHA (1996)).

Other information useful in identifying hazards and hazardous materials include piping and instrumentation diagrams, process flow diagrams, plot plans, topographic maps, utility system drawings, and major types of process equipment, etc.

The nature and extent of hazards is affected by process conditions and the interactions that can occur between hazardous materials. Therefore, information about these interactions should also be taken into account in identifying hazards. A systematic approach for addressing these issues might make use of an "interaction matrix" [see Section 3.3, AIChE (1992)]. An example of this technique for the ammonium diuranate (ADU) process at a nuclear fuel fabrication facility is given in Appendix B.4. Such a matrix indicates incompatibilities among various materials used in the process that could result in potential accidents. Several of the ISA methods listed in Section 2.3 could also be used to facilitate the hazard identification process. These include Safety Review, Checklist Analysis, Relative Ranking, Preliminary Hazard Analysis, and What-If Analysis.

At a minimum, the results of the hazard identification process should document radioactive materials, fissile materials, flammable materials, toxic materials, hazardous reactions, and hazardous process conditions. The documentation should include maximum intended inventory amounts and the location of the hazardous materials on-site. In addition, the hazards (i.e, radiological, chemical, etc.) of each process in the facility should be identified.

2.6.4 Performing the Hazard Analysis

Each ISA hazard analysis method is performed in its own unique fashion. HAZOP, for example, concentrates on process upset conditions whereas FMEA examines the failures of equipment and components. The goal of all methods, however, is to identify possible accident sequences and the controls needed to prevent or limit their occurrence or mitigate the consequences.

2.6.4.1 Preparation

Despite differences in the various methods, certain aspects of the ISA process are generally applicable. First, the preparation for the ISA should be thorough (i.e., the team should be selected, a schedule developed, information gathered and distributed, the process divided into sections, and a methodology for recording information developed). The team should be aware of the scope of the evaluation and the objectives of the analysis. The leader should give an overview of the ISA method to the team in order that they know what procedure will be used and how it is carried out. The leader should stress that the team's primary role is initially one of problem identification rather than problem solving.

2.6.4.2 Team meetings

The ability to perform a successful analysis is dependent on the effectiveness of team meetings and the capabilities of the team leader. It is important that an atmosphere conducive to free and open expression is maintained so that the team members can fully engage themselves in the ISA process. The meetings need to be kept on track so that the analysis is systematically performed, section by section.

If, during the team meetings, documentation is found to be out-of-date, or other information is needed to complete the analysis, then updated or more complete information should be provided or developed. The responsibility for these tasks needs to be assigned to appropriate team members. Once the new information has been compiled, additional meetings may be necessary to consider the implication of the new information.

For each of the methods identified earlier (Section 2.3 of this document), Chapter 6 of AIChE (1992) provides information on how to perform an analysis using that approach, and the results that can be obtained. In addition, part II of AIChE (1992) provides a description of how each method is applied to a fictional but realistic process. The description includes a dramatization, of team meetings, that gives the reader a good understanding of how the meetings and the analyses are actually performed.

2.6.4.3 Integration

ISA, as the name implies, is intended to provide an "integrated" analysis of facility hazards. That is, the analysis should take into account interactions among different types of hazards. For example, the release and ignition of an explosive material (chemical/fire hazard) could affect the release of radioactive materials (radiological hazard). Indeed, the controls (sprinkler system) used to protect against one hazard (fire) may increase the likelihood of an accident involving a different hazard (criticality). The ISA should take into account the interactions of various hazards and controls, to ensure that the combination of controls proposed to address multiple hazards assures an acceptable level of overall risk.

The integration of ISA results is likely to be fostered by a process that encourages a simultaneous consideration of all types of process hazards. This approach would allow the multidisciplinary team to discuss the optimization of controls needed to prevent or mitigate all process accidents identified. An alternative approach would be to conduct separate analyses for each of the types of hazards (i.e., radiological, chemical, fire, and criticality) and assemble the entire ISA team for the purpose of optimizing and integrating the findings of these studies.

The effort at integration of analysis results also applies to the case where the overall system analysis has been arbitrarily divided into several smaller sub-system analyses, to reduce complexity. In this case, care must be taken to avoid the inadvertent omission of domino or cascading effects. For example, a fire in one subsystem may spread to a second subsystem causing a release of toxic material. Each subsystem analysis should take into account the input and output of materials and energy that can affect and be affected by the other subsystems. Appendix C illustrates a situation involving a system that has been divided into three subsystems, each with varying degrees of interaction among them.

17

2.6.5 Results of the Analysis

The results of an ISA consist of an identification of potential accidents, the consequences of the accidents and their likelihood of occurrence, and the controls (i.e., the structures, systems, equipment, components, and actions of personnel) relied on to prevent the accidents from occurring or to reduce their consequences.

2.6.5.1 Accident Sequences

Although the formats for recording the results of an ISA differ depending on the method used (see Chapter 6 of AIChE (1992)), the essential information obtained is a description of potential accident sequences. (An accident sequence is "a specific unplanned sequence of events that results in an undesirable consequence.") Therefore, an important product of an ISA consists of a description of all accident sequences identified and recorded during the analysis process. An accident sequence involves an initiating event, any factors that allow the accident to propagate (enablers), and any factors that reduce the risk (likelihood or consequence) of the accident (controls). The accident sequence is a sequence of specific real events. The initiating event is often the failure of some device or feature of the process that is an item relied on for safety. Such events are sometimes process upsets, but the frequency of such upsets is almost always controlled by features of the design or by operating procedures. Hence, these process features are being relied on for safety. Alternatively the initiating event could be a challenge from outside the system, that is, an external event. For an initiating event to lead to the consequences of concern it must usually be above a certain level of severity. For example, excursions of process parameters beyond normal conditions may be an upset, but if within safety limits, there is no chance of further progression. The subsequent events in the accident sequence are usually failures of hardware controls or manual procedures to limit or prevent damage. Like initiating events, failures of these controls must be of sufficient severity to permit progression of the accident to actual consequences of concern. Thus failure is a question of degree. The ISA should clearly describe this sequence of events which leads to the accident.

Table 1.3 from AIChE (1992) provides a list of possible initiating events, propagating events, risk reduction factors (controls), and incident outcomes. The initiating events can be categorized as process upsets, management system failures, human errors, and external events (e.g, high winds, floods). Propagating events include equipment failure, ignition sources, management system failure, human error, domino effects (other containment failures or material releases), and external conditions. Risk reduction factors include control/operator responses, safety system responses, mitigation system responses, and emergency plan responses, etc.

2.6.5.2 Consequences and Likelihoods

In addition to the description of the accident sequence, an estimate of the consequences resulting from the accident should be described in the ISA. If the sequence would result in a release of radioactive material, or if a criticality would occur, the dose to the nearest member of the public should be estimated[4]. If uranium is released in soluble form, the intake by the nearest member of the public should be estimated. If HF (produced by the reaction of UF_6 with moist air) is released, the intake of HF should be estimated. Similar estimates should be made for the exposure of workers. An efficient way to estimate consequences of the accidents identified is to review the results of preliminary consequence analyses for prototype accidents for each type of hazard. Particularly useful as prototypes are consequence analyses at bounding, but physically possible, conditions leading to maximal consequences. Comparing the hazardous material inventory, and other conditions, for the prototype to the inventory for the accident identified can permit a quick estimate of its consequences by extrapolation.

These consequence estimates are needed to determine the level of control needed to protect against the occurrence of the accident. If the health effects exceed the consequences of concern (Section 2.6.1.1, "Consequences of Concern"), then the controls that are used must provide reasonable assurance that such unmitigated consequences will not take place. The degree of assurance should be commensurate with the potential consequences. Part 70 requires sufficient controls to ensure that the occurrence of any high consequence event is "highly unlikely" and the occurrence of any intermediate consequence event is "unlikely." The ability to meet these conditions requires that licensees estimate the likelihood of occurrence of potential accidents identified in the ISA.

2.6.5.3 Safety Controls

One of the most important results obtained from the ISA is the identification of the controls needed to ensure the safe operation of the facility. In 10 CFR Part 70, Subpart H, safety controls are referred to by the more generic phrase: "items relied on for safety (IROFS)." These items relied on for safety are defined as: "structures, systems, equipment, components, and activities of personnel that are relied on to prevent potential accidents...". In this document safety controls and items relied on for safety are synonymous. Safety controls used at a facility can be characterized as either administrative or engineered. Administrative controls are generally not considered to be as reliable as engineered controls since human errors usually occur more frequently than equipment failures (AIChE, 1992). Engineered controls may be categorized as being "passive" or "active." Passive controls include pipes or vessels that provide containment. Active controls include equipment such as pumps or valves that perform a specific function related to safety. In general, passive controls are considered to be less prone to failure than active controls.

The ISA process by itself cannot ensure the effective design and implementation of the controls, and their proper operation. Instead, other elements of the licensee's safety program are relied on to provide this assurance. For example, as part of the measures used to ensure criticality, radiological, chemical, and fire safety, design criteria for relevant safety controls are established.

---

[4]Further guidance on the calculation of consequences will be provided in the chemical safety and radiological safety chapters of the Standard Review Plan (SRP) and in the "Nuclear Fuel Cycle Facility Accident Analysis Handbook (U.S Nuclear Regulatory Commission, 1998).

(The controls identified in the ISA should adhere to these criteria.) Quality Assurance (QA) measures should ensure that the safety controls implemented at the plant satisfy the design criteria. Training measures should confirm that the personnel called on to operate or interact with the controls are properly trained. Maintenance and equipment inspection measures should ensure that the engineered controls are reliable and maintained in proper working order. Audits and inspections are conducted to determine whether standard operating procedures are being followed.

In choosing the controls needed to protect against the occurrence of a particular event sequence, both the number and the effectiveness of such controls should be taken into account. For engineered controls, in addition to their inherent effectiveness, maintenance, calibration, and surveillance measures provide assurance that the controls are in place and in working order. Depending on the degree to which a particular control is relied on (i.e., whether it is the only control or one of several redundant controls), maintenance measures should be appropriately graded to that specific control. Similarly, for administrative controls, training measures and audit/inspection measures should be tailored to ensure the specific reliability needed for each control. For example, if the facility is relying on a single individual on duty at a particular time to take action (i.e., close a valve or turn a switch) to avoid a major accident, that person should receive special training and the person's performance should be carefully monitored. In addition, the man-machine interface for that individual should be carefully designed. All of this information is necessary to provide a clear understanding of the controls used in the process, and their effectiveness.

In summary, to provide reasonable assurance that a particular accident sequence will not occur, the licensee/applicant should not only identify the control(s) that have been implemented, but also reference the specific features of its safety program (i.e., training, quality assurance, maintenance, calibration, and surveillance, etc.) that ensure the reliability of those controls.

2.6.6 Documenting the ISA Results

Subpart H of Part 70 requires certain licensees to document the performance and results of the ISA process to demonstrate that it was conducted using sound practices and that it comprehensively identifies the structures, systems, equipment, components, and personnel relied on for safe operations. Documentation of the ISA is also important in supporting good risk management decisions and in supporting other safety program activities such as maintaining accurate standard operating procedures, managing change (configuration management), investigating incidents, and conducting audits and inspections, etc. Finally, documentation is necessary to consolidate and maintain the results of the study for future use.

The ISA documentation should include not only the results of the analysis (i.e., the description of accident sequences), but other information related to the conduct of the ISA. The amount of information used and generated during the ISA process can be substantial. The process safety information alone can include many detailed drawings and diagrams as well as hundreds of pages of specifications, procedures, etc. In addition to the process safety information, the documentation of the ISA should include a description of the site, the facility, the processes that were analyzed, the method that was used, the people who performed the analysis, the time frame during which the analysis was performed, the potential accident sequences that were identified, and the safety controls and associated management controls that have been identified and implemented to prevent or mitigate the consequences of the identified accidents. The important assumptions made in the analysis should also be documented. All documentation associated with the ISA process should be maintained by the licensee's Configuration Management System to assure that it is representative of the current status of the facility.

The information submitted for NRC review along with a license or license renewal application is expected to be a subset of the entire ISA documentation. This information is described in the "Standard Review Plan for the Review of a License Application for a Fuel Cycle Facility," draft NUREG-1520. The Standard Review Plan will also address the role of the Configuration Management System in maintaining control of the ISA documentation.

2.6.6.1 Site Description

A description of the site should be provided including information on site meteorology, seismology, topography, demography, and any other factors that have safety significance.

2.6.6.2 Facility Description

The objective of this description is to define the boundaries of the analysis and identify those facility-specific factors that could have a bearing on potential accidents and their consequences.

The description should include the location of the facility, and the presence of nearby activities or structures, such as factories, railroads, airports, and dams, etc., that could pose a hazard to the facility. It should also include the number of workers in the work force and the different skills needed for operation. In addition, it should include the location of all of the buildings at the facility and their relationship to the licensed operation.

2.6.6.3 Process Description

The documentation of the ISA should contain a description of each process analyzed. This should include:

- a discussion of the basic theory that the process is based on,

- a discussion of the function of major components used in the process and a summary of normal process operations,

- a summary of the dimensions, materials, and configuration of lines and vessels used in the process, and

- a reference list of system documents (i.e., drawings, procedures, etc.) used to perform the ISA.

2.6.6.4 ISA Methods

The documentation should identify, for each unit process analyzed, the method or methods chosen to perform each of the tasks of the ISA, including hazard analysis (accident identification), likelihood evaluation, and consequence evaluation. In particular, the flowchart of Appendix A should be used to select a hazard analysis method. If the method indicated by applying Appendix A is not selected the basis on which the choice was made should be justified. References should be cited for descriptions of standard methods used. If the facility uses non-standard methods, they should be adequately documented.

2.6.6.5 ISA Team

The documentation should identify the members of the team used to perform the ISA and should explain the basis on which the choice was made. The experience and qualifications of team members should be included.

2.6.6.6 Accident Sequences

The documentation should include a description of accident sequences identified in the analysis, the consequences of those accidents, and the likelihood of those accidents. For those accidents that have consequences that exceed the levels identified in Section 2.6.1.1. ("Consequences of Concern"), the information provided should also specifically address the initiating event, any factors that allow the accident to propagate, and any factors that reduce the risk of the accident.

2.6.6.7 Controls

Because the implementation of controls and their effectiveness is crucial to the safety of the facility, documentation of the ISA process should include a list of safety controls (i.e, structures, systems, equipment, components, and personnel relied upon for safety) used in each process and, for each, the associated management controls (i.e., QA, maintenance, training, etc.) used to ensure its appropriate functioning.

3 REFERENCES

N.W. Knox and R.W. Eicher, <u>MORT Users Manual</u>, SSDC-4 (Revision 2), U.S. Department of Energy, Idaho Falls, ID, 1983.

W.G. Johnson, <u>MORT Safety Assurance Systems</u>, Marcel Dekker, New York, 1980.

W.G. Johnson, <u>MORT, the Management Oversight and Risk Tree</u>, U.S. Atomic Energy Commission, Washington D.C., 1973.

<u>Guidelines for Chemical Process Quantitative Risk Analysis</u>, Center for Chemical Process Safety, AIChE, New York, 1989.

<u>Guidelines for Hazard Evaluation Procedures, Second Edition with Worked Examples</u>, Center for Chemical Process Safety, AIChE, New York, 1992.

NUREG-1520, "Standard Review Plan for the Review of a License Application for a Fuel Cycle Facility," U.S. Nuclear Regulatory Commission [DRAFT] May 11, 2000.

American Petroleum Institute, <u>Management of Process Hazards, Recommended Practice 750,</u> First Edition, Washington D.C., 1990.

Chemical Manufacturers Association, Inc., <u>Responsible Care Resources,</u> Washington D.C., January 1992.

New Jersey Toxic Catastrophe Prevention Act, January 1986.

California Acutely Hazardous Materials: Risk Management Act, September 1986.

Delaware Extremely Hazardous Substances Risk Management Act, July 1988.

Nevada Highly Hazardous Substance Act, July 1991.

Occupational Safety and Health Administration Process Safety Management Regulations (29 CFR 1910.119) 1991.

"U.S. Environmental Protection Agency Risk Management Program for Chemical Accidental Release Prevention," Proposed Rule, <u>Federal Register,</u> Vol. 58, No. 201, 1993.

U.S. Department of Energy, Order 5480.23, "Nuclear Safety Analysis Reports," April 10, 1992, updated March 10, 1994.

U.S. Nuclear Regulatory Commission, "Nuclear Fuel Cycle Facility Accident Analysis Handbook," NUREG/CR-6410, March 1998.

U.S. Nuclear Regulatory Commission, 10 CFR 70, Domestic Licensing of Special Nuclear Material; Possession of a Critical Mass of Special Nuclear Material, Federal Register Vol. 65, No. 181, page 56211, September 18, 2000.

APPENDIX A

Flowchart for Selecting a Hazards Analysis Technique

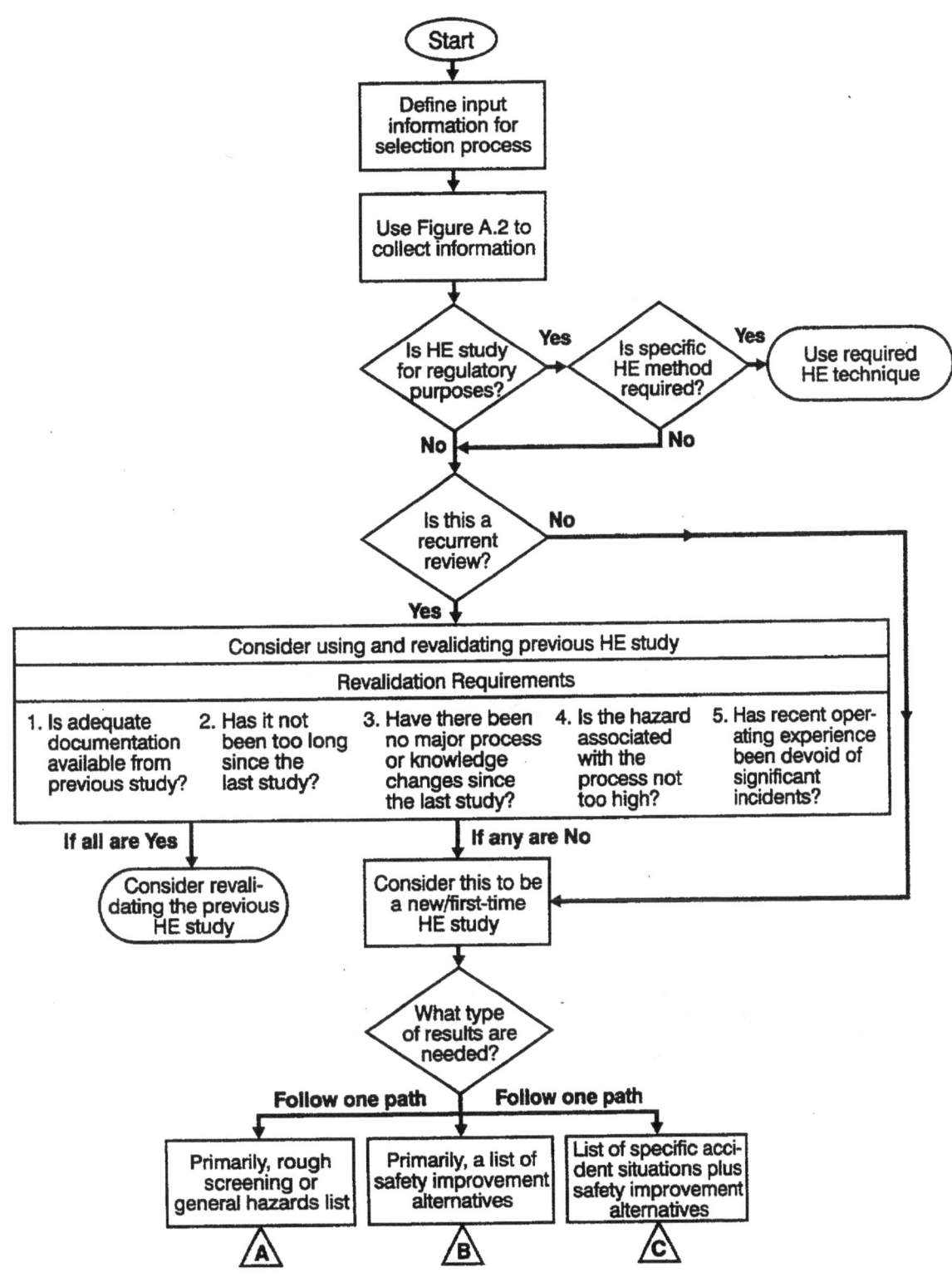

Figure A.1. Example flowchart for selecting an HE technique.

A-1

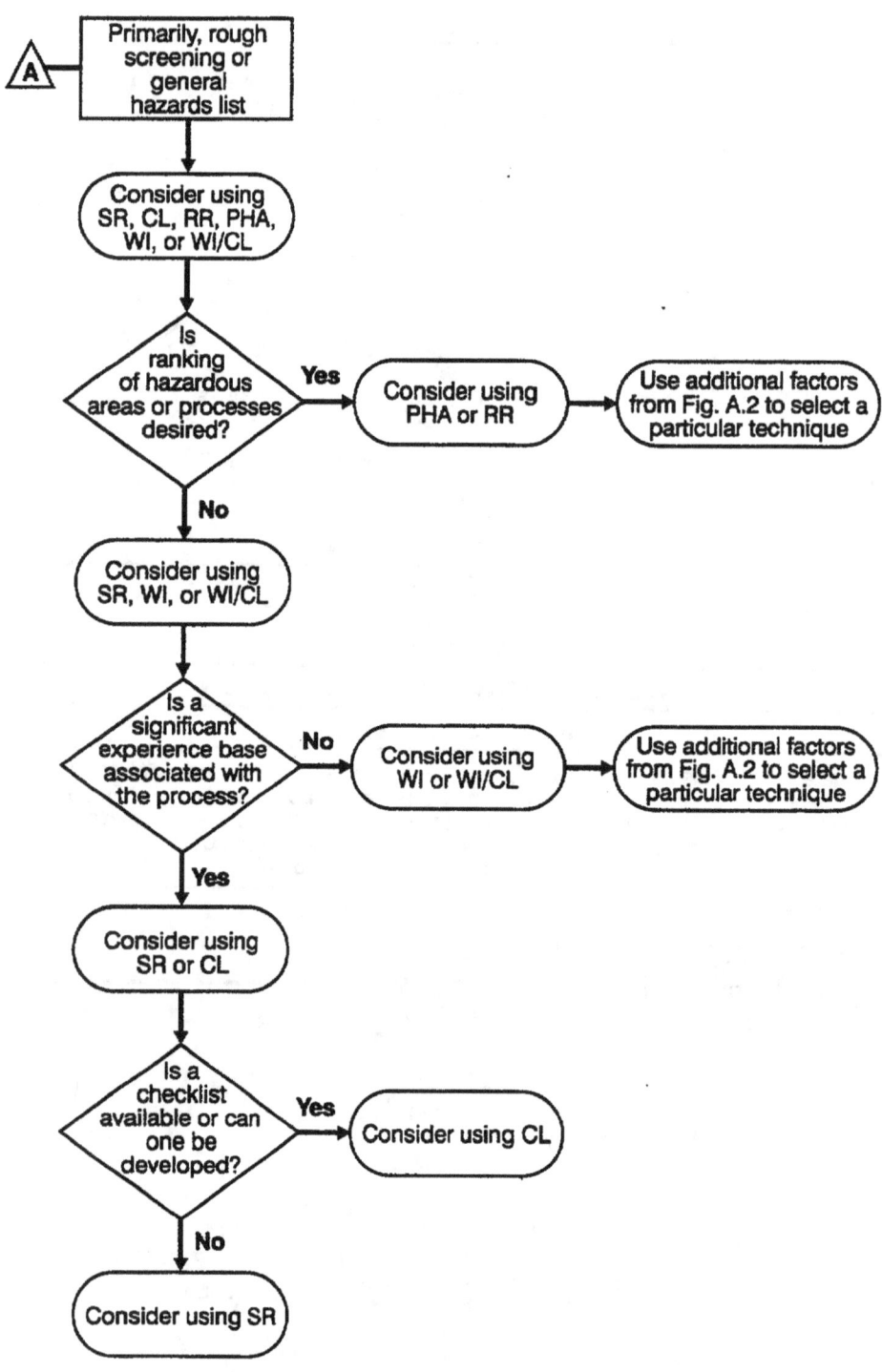

Example flowchart for selecting an HE technique. (Cont.)

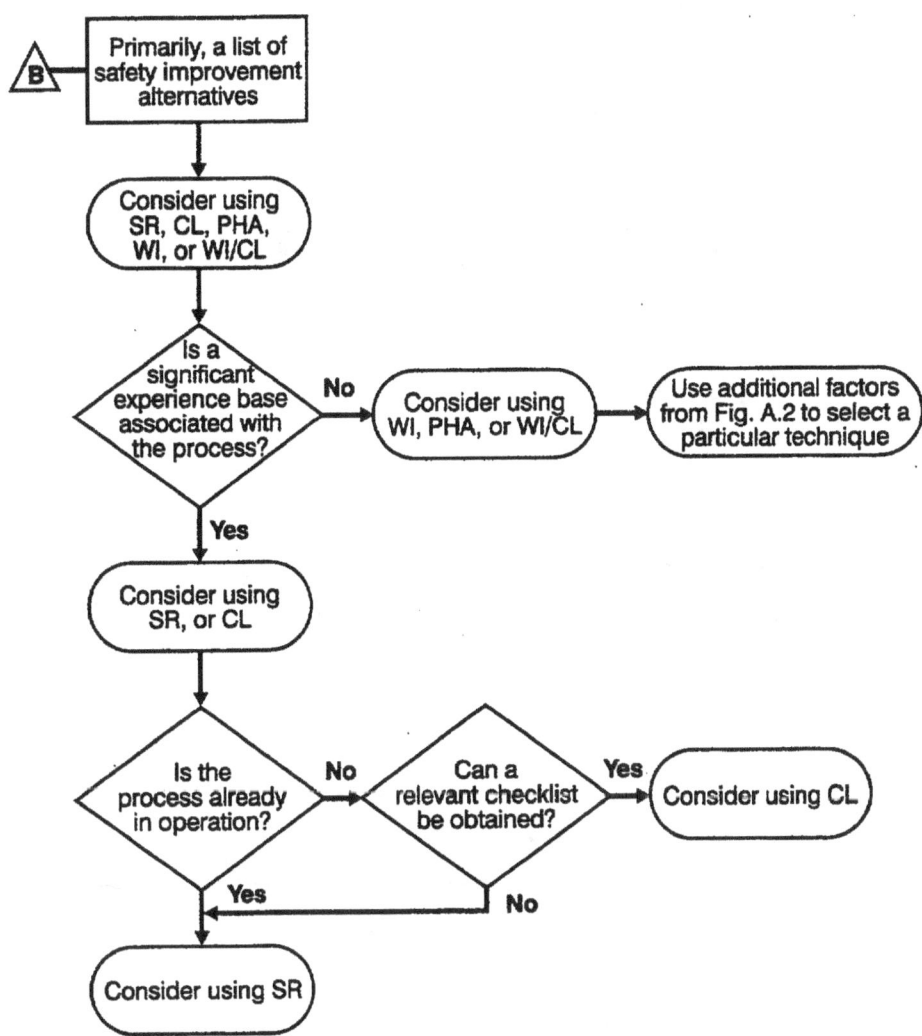

Example flowchart for selecting an HE technique. (Cont.)

A-3

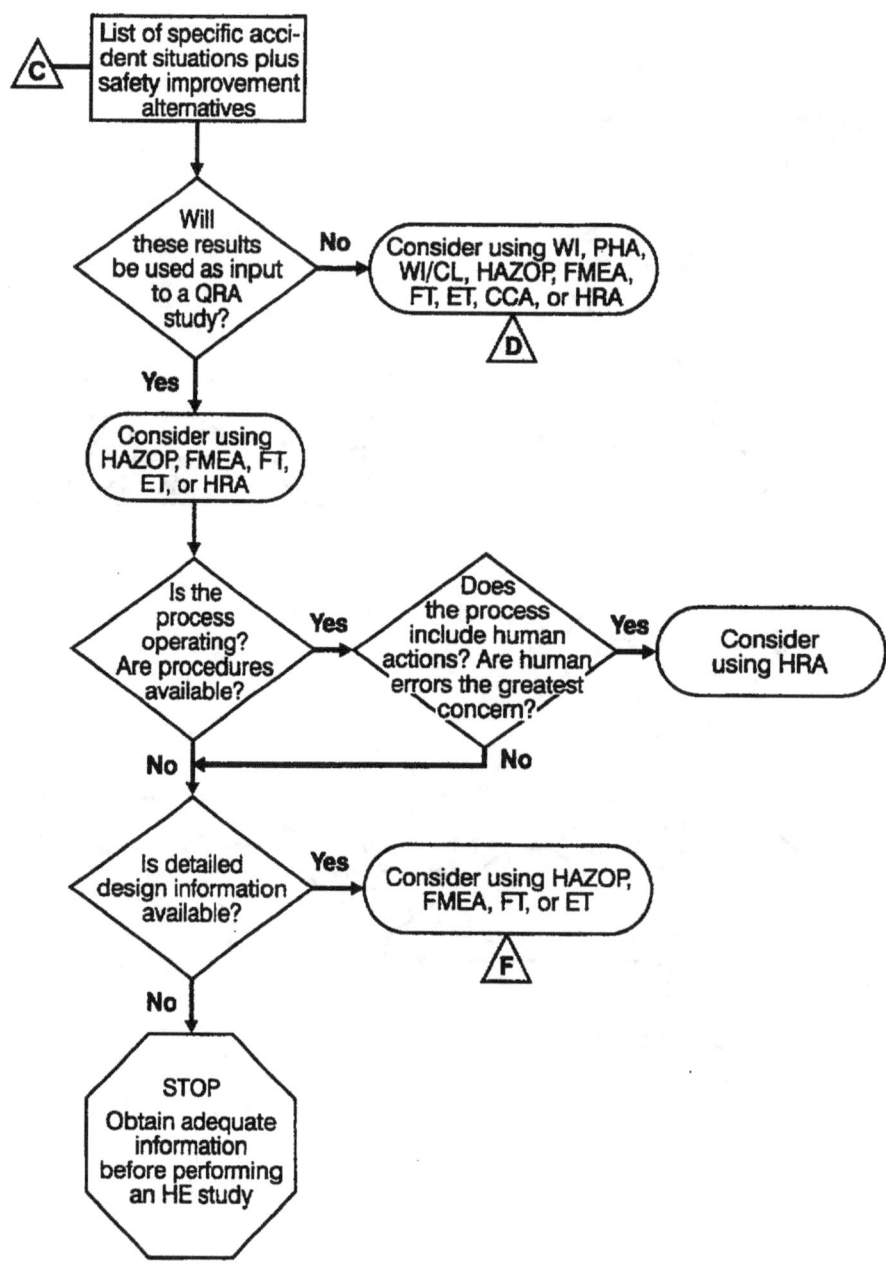

Example flowchart for selecting an HE technique. (Cont.)

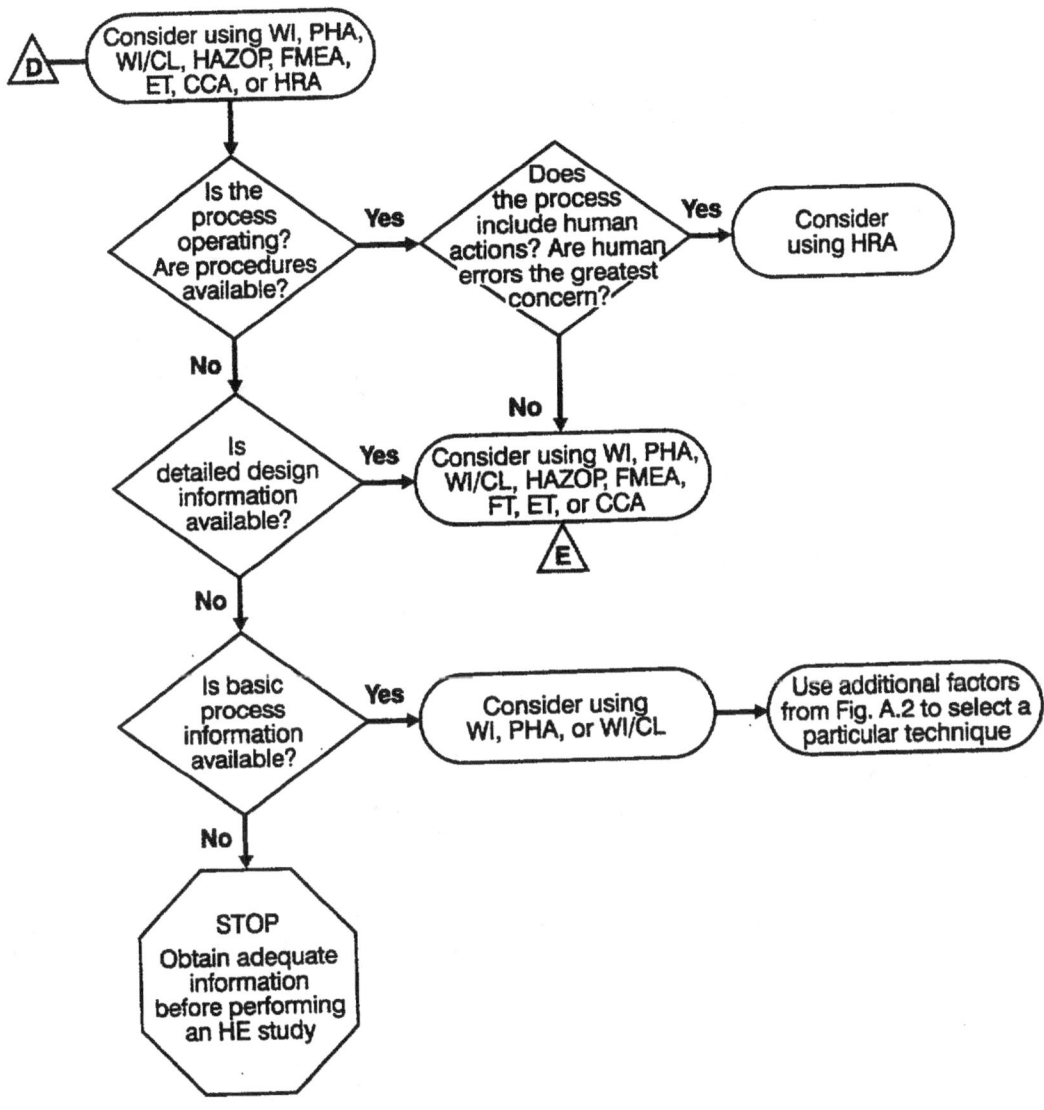

Example flowchart for selecting an HE technique. (Cont.)

A-5

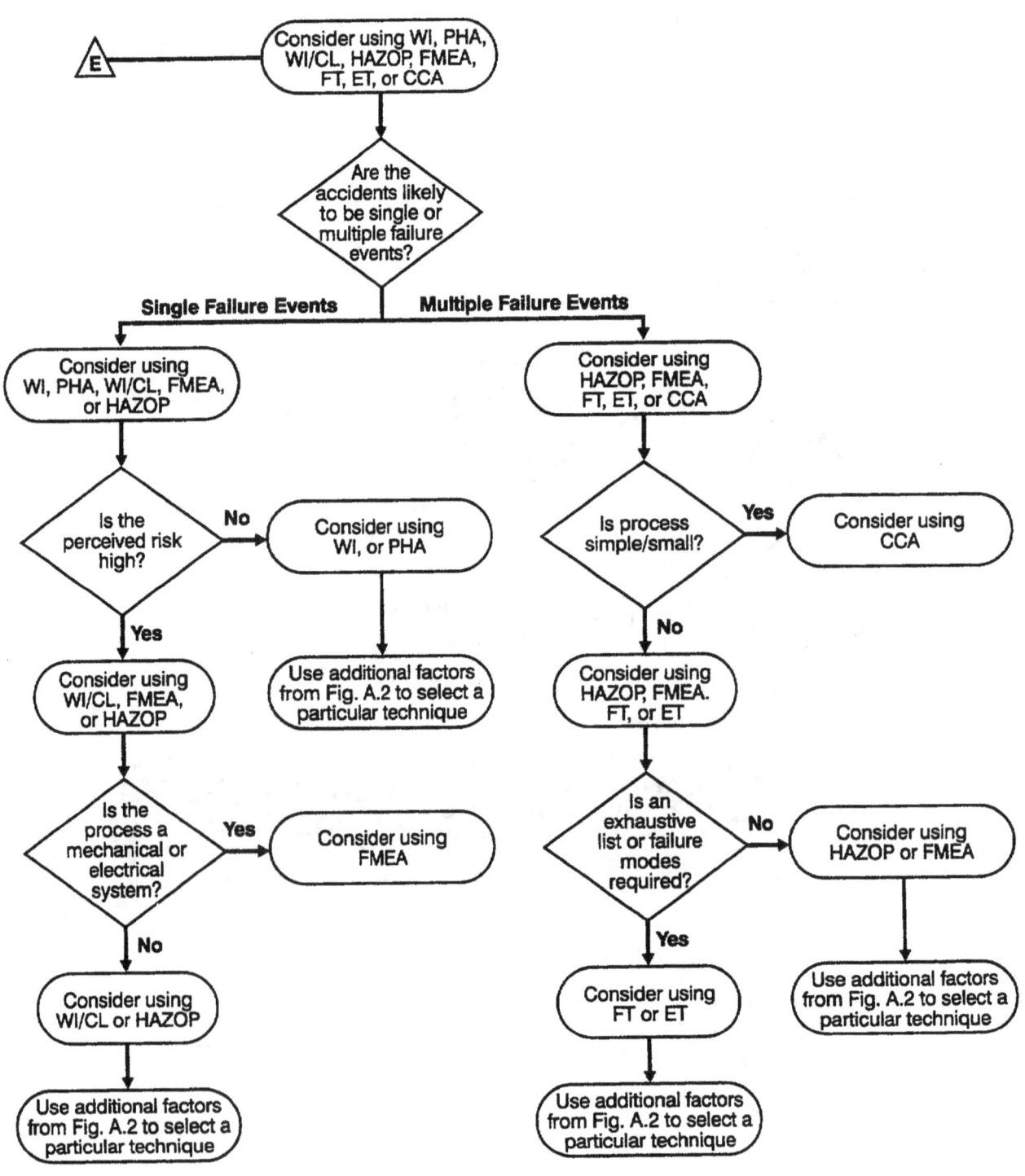

Example flowchart for selecting an HE technique. (Cont.)

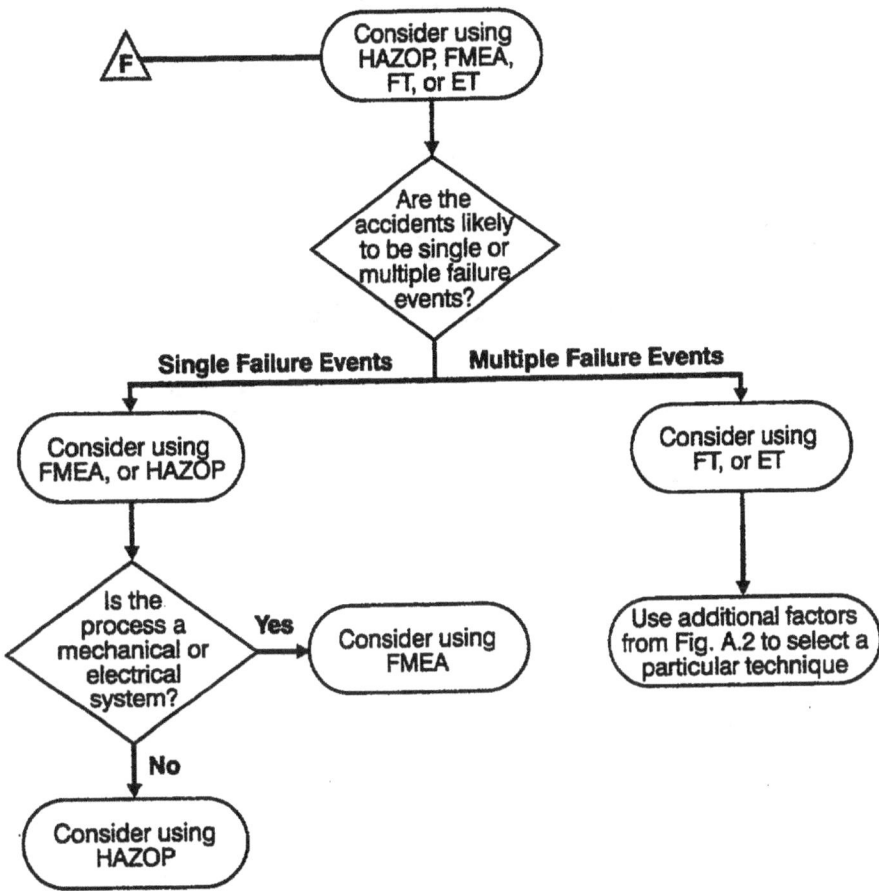

Example flowchart for selecting an HE technique. (Cont.)

Abbreviations:

HE = hazard evaluation

SR = safety review

CL = checklist analysis

RR = relative ranking

PHA = preliminary hazard analysis

WI = what=if analysis

WI/CL = what=if/checklist analysis

HAZOP = hazard and operability analysis

FMEA = failure modes and effects analysis

ET = event tree analysis

FT = fault tree analysis

CCA = cause-consequence analysis

HRA = human reliability analysis

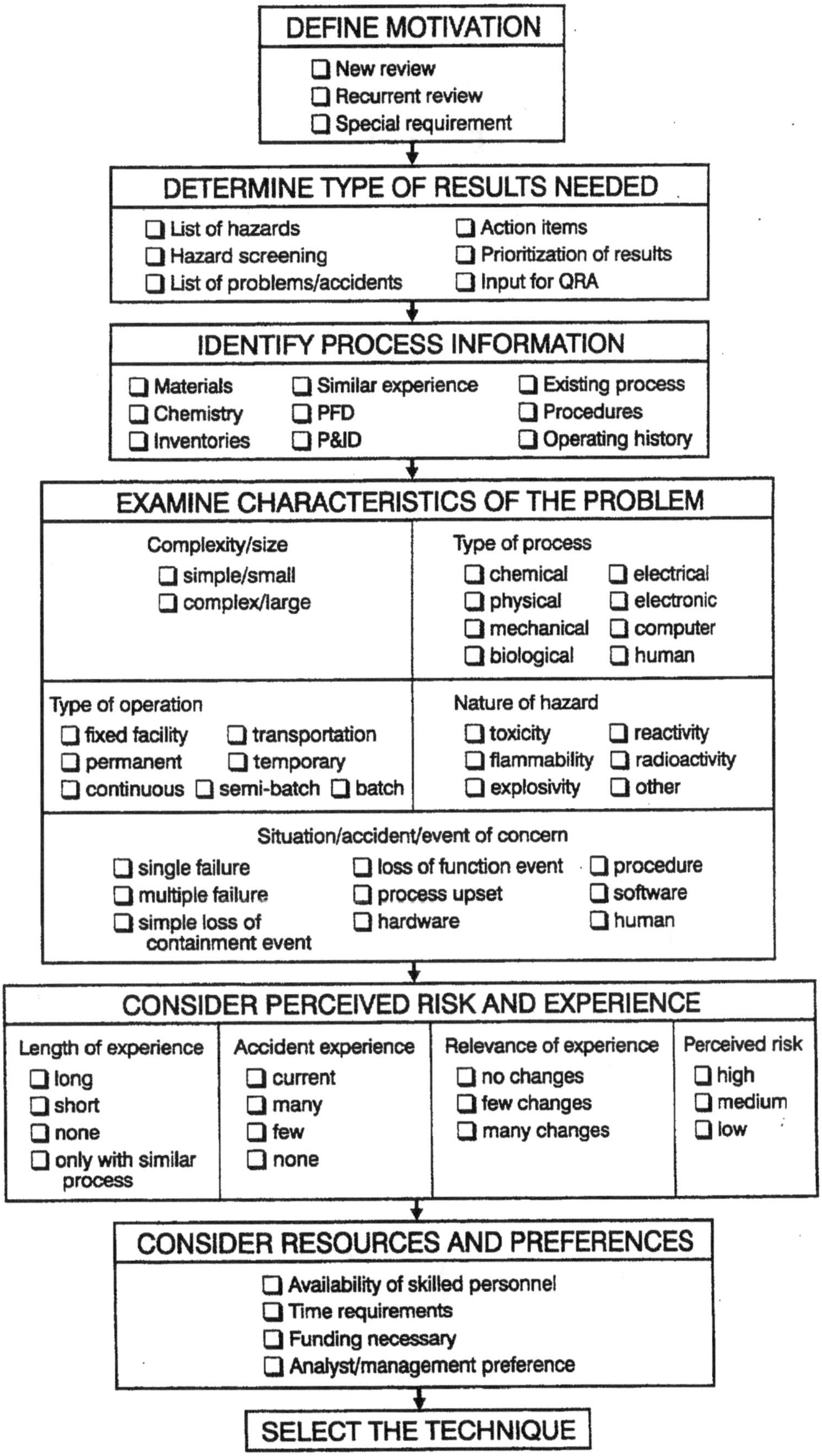

DEFINE MOTIVATION

- ❏ New review
- ❏ Recurrent review
- ❏ Special requirement

DETERMINE TYPE OF RESULTS NEEDED

- ❏ List of hazards
- ❏ Hazard screening
- ❏ List of problems/accidents
- ❏ Action items
- ❏ Prioritization of results
- ❏ Input for QRA

IDENTIFY PROCESS INFORMATION

- ❏ Materials
- ❏ Chemistry
- ❏ Inventories
- ❏ Similar experience
- ❏ PFD
- ❏ P&ID
- ❏ Existing process
- ❏ Procedures
- ❏ Operating history

EXAMINE CHARACTERISTICS OF THE PROBLEM

Complexity/size
- ❏ simple/small
- ❏ complex/large

Type of process
- ❏ chemical
- ❏ physical
- ❏ mechanical
- ❏ biological
- ❏ electrical
- ❏ electronic
- ❏ computer
- ❏ human

Type of operation
- ❏ fixed facility
- ❏ permanent
- ❏ continuous
- ❏ transportation
- ❏ temporary
- ❏ semi-batch ❏ batch

Nature of hazard
- ❏ toxicity
- ❏ flammability
- ❏ explosivity
- ❏ reactivity
- ❏ radioactivity
- ❏ other

Situation/accident/event of concern
- ❏ single failure
- ❏ multiple failure
- ❏ simple loss of containment event
- ❏ loss of function event
- ❏ process upset
- ❏ hardware
- ❏ procedure
- ❏ software
- ❏ human

CONSIDER PERCEIVED RISK AND EXPERIENCE

Length of experience
- ❏ long
- ❏ short
- ❏ none
- ❏ only with similar process

Accident experience
- ❏ current
- ❏ many
- ❏ few
- ❏ none

Relevance of experience
- ❏ no changes
- ❏ few changes
- ❏ many changes

Perceived risk
- ❏ high
- ❏ medium
- ❏ low

CONSIDER RESOURCES AND PREFERENCES

- ❏ Availability of skilled personnel
- ❏ Time requirements
- ❏ Funding necessary
- ❏ Analyst/management preference

SELECT THE TECHNIQUE

Figure A.2. Criteria for selecting HE techniques.

A-9

APPENDIX B

Application of ISA to Nuclear Fuel Cycle Processes

B.1 What-If Analysis of the Pelletizing, Rod-loading, and Fuel Bundle Assembly Steps

In this example, the what-if method is used to study criticality hazards in a uranium fuel fabrication operation. The process, shown in Figure B-1, begins with a roll-type compaction unit that takes uranium oxide (UO_2) powder and binder-lubricant and combines it before feeding to the pellet presses where pellets are formed. The pellets are transferred in boats to the sintering furnace, where the pellets are sintered in a hydrogen atmosphere to 95 percent theoretical density. The pellets are then ground to precise dimensions, and dried. Dried and inspected pellets are loaded into empty fuel tubes that are pressurized and sealed. Finished fuel rods are bundled into assemblies and stored.

In the following analysis, it is assumed that the prevention of an inadvertent criticality is accomplished by preventing the presence of excess moderating material and by maintaining appropriate geometric controls.

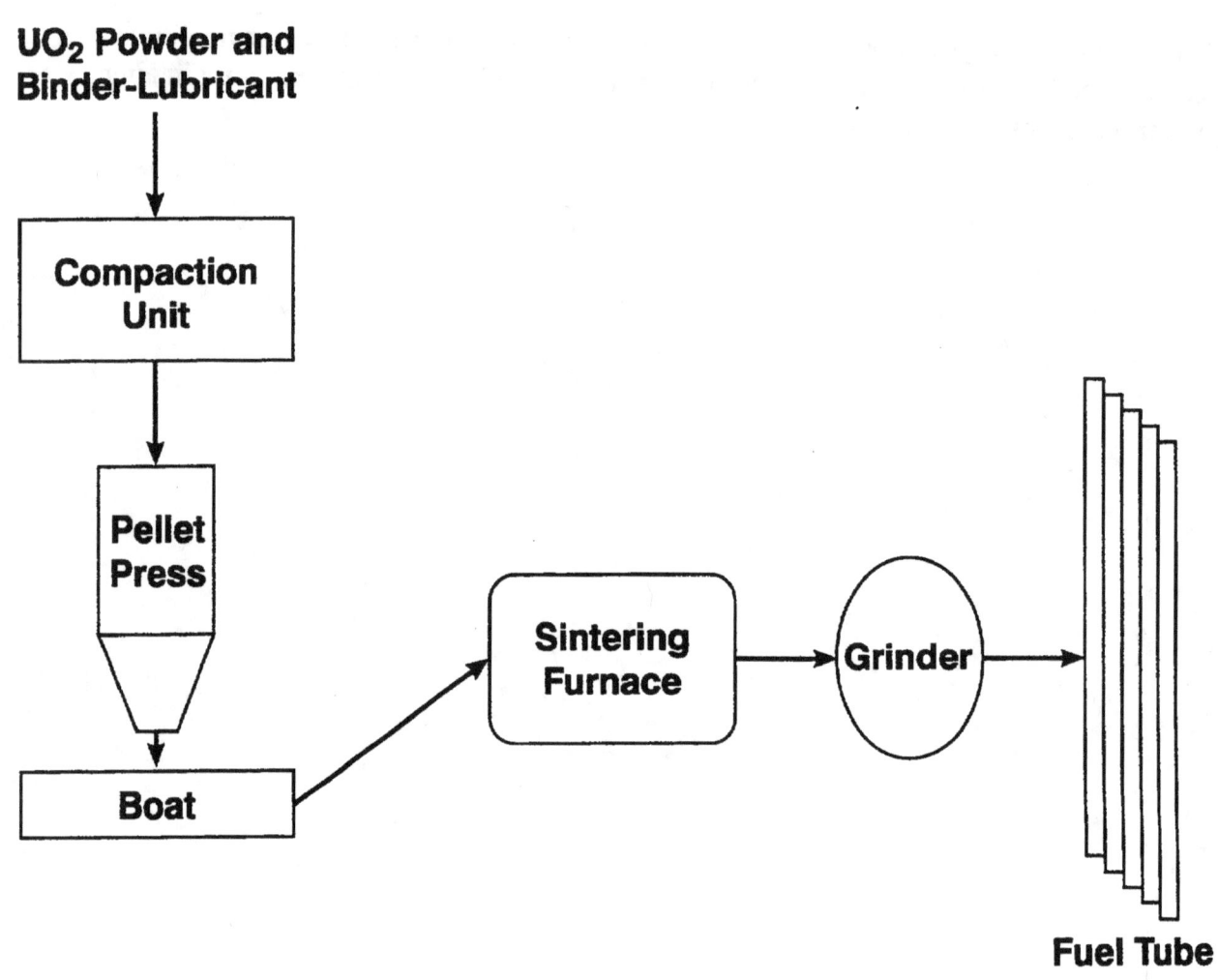

Figure B.1. Uranium Fuel Fabrication

What-If Analysis of Pelletizing Step

Subject: Criticality

What-If/Cause	Consequence/Hazard	Safeguards
Moderation Control Fails Because:		
Hydraulic fluid leaks.	Moderator reaches powder/criticality.	All hydraulic fluid systems are shielded from powder.
Powder is not dry enough.	Moderator reaches powder/criticality.	Multiple quality control steps for analytical results.
Room floods.	Moderator reaches powder/criticality.	No piped water systems in bulk powder handling areas.
Bulk powder storage container collects and holds liquid.	Moderator reaches powder/criticality.	Bulk containers are moved with sealed opening facing down.
Geometry Control Fails Because:		
Cart tips over.	Safe geometry exceeded/criticality.	Passive stops welded to bottom of carts.
Powder builds up in pelletizing equipment.	Safe geometry exceeded/criticality.	Buildup prevention devises within equipment.
Small powder storage container breaks.	Safe geometry exceeded/criticality.	Containers are of rugged construction, containers are administratively protected.
Sintering boats are stacked too high.	Safe geometry exceeded/criticality.	Training, administrative controls

What-If Analysis of Fuel Rod Loading and Bundle Assembly Steps

Subject: Criticality

What-If/Cause	Consequence/Hazard	Safeguards
Moderation Control Fails Because:		
Assembly shroud collects moderator.	Moderator reaches rods/criticality.	Shrouds are split to prevent accumulation.
Room floods.	Moderator reaches rods/criticality.	No piped water systems in bulk powder handling areas.
Geometry Control Fails Because:		
Stored fuel rods are stacked.	Safe geometry exceeded/criticality.	Storage and transport containers have controlled thickness, only one channel of rods may be transported at a time, administrative controls and training.
Assemblies are stored too close.	Safe geometry exceeded/ criticality.	Storage racks control spacing.
Assemblies are spaced too closely during cleaning.	Safe geometry exceeded/ criticality.	Wash tanks have spacers to control distance.
Rods dissolve during cleaning step.	Safe geometry exceeded/ criticality.	Wash tank contents are strictly controlled.
Poison inserted to supplement geometry is removed.	Safe geometry exceeded/ criticality.	Boral shelves are fixed inside carts.

B.2 Hazard and Operability Analysis of the Vaporization Step of UF$_6$ Dry Conversion

In this example, the Hazard and Operability Analysis (HAZOP) Method is used to model the hazards in a uranium hexafuoride (UF$_6$) dry conversion process. The process is depicted in the following figure. In the process, UF$_6$ gas is converted to a dry powder. The UF$_6$ gas arrives in a large steel cylinder that is loaded into a horizontal vaporizer chest, heated by circulating hot water sprays. The vaporized UF$_6$ and superheated steam are then introduced to a slab-shaped disentrainment chamber at the feed end of a conversion kiln. Here they undergo dry hydrolysis to form uranyl fluoride (UO$_2$F$_2$) powder and hydrogen fluoride (HF) gas. The powder falls to the chamber bottom and is continuously removed to the discharge end of the kiln. Hydrogen (H$_2$) gas and superheated steam are fed to the kiln discharge end to strip the fluoride and reduce the powder to uranium dioxide (UO$_2$). H$_2$, HF, nitrogen (N$_2$), and steam are continuously removed from the kiln through process filters. Product powder is continuously removed into a UO$_2$ check-hopper, which is nitrogen-purged.

The first step in the HAZOP process is to apply guide words to process parameters, as illustrated below for "Pressure."

Process Section:	Vessel - Vaporizer Steam Chest
Design Intention:	Vaporize UF$_6$
Guide Word:	High
Process Parameter:	Pressure
Deviation:	High Pressure in UF$_6$ cylinder
Consequences:	1) Potential criticality concern
	2) Release of UF$_6$ to vaporizer and atmosphere
Causes:	1) Low/no flow in emergency cooling water
	2) Overfilled cylinder
Safeguards:	1) High pressure indicator and alarm
	2) Administrative controls

The steps are then repeated for additional parameters and guide words, and the results tabulated in the HAZOP Study Table (Table B-1). Note that only the vaporization step in the dry conversion process has been included in the table.

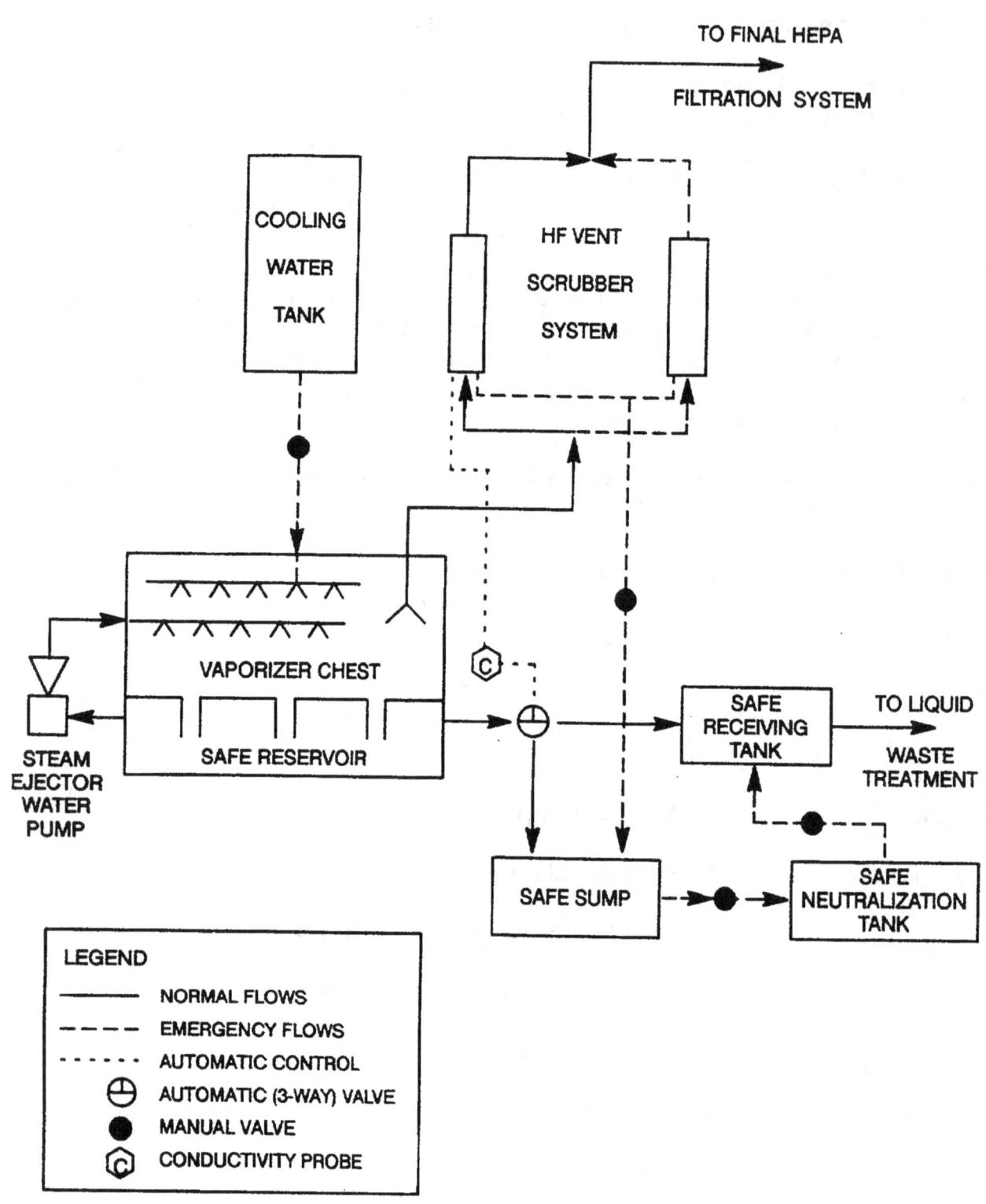

Figure B.2

UF$_6$ Dry Conversion Process
Vaporization Operation Waste Handling System

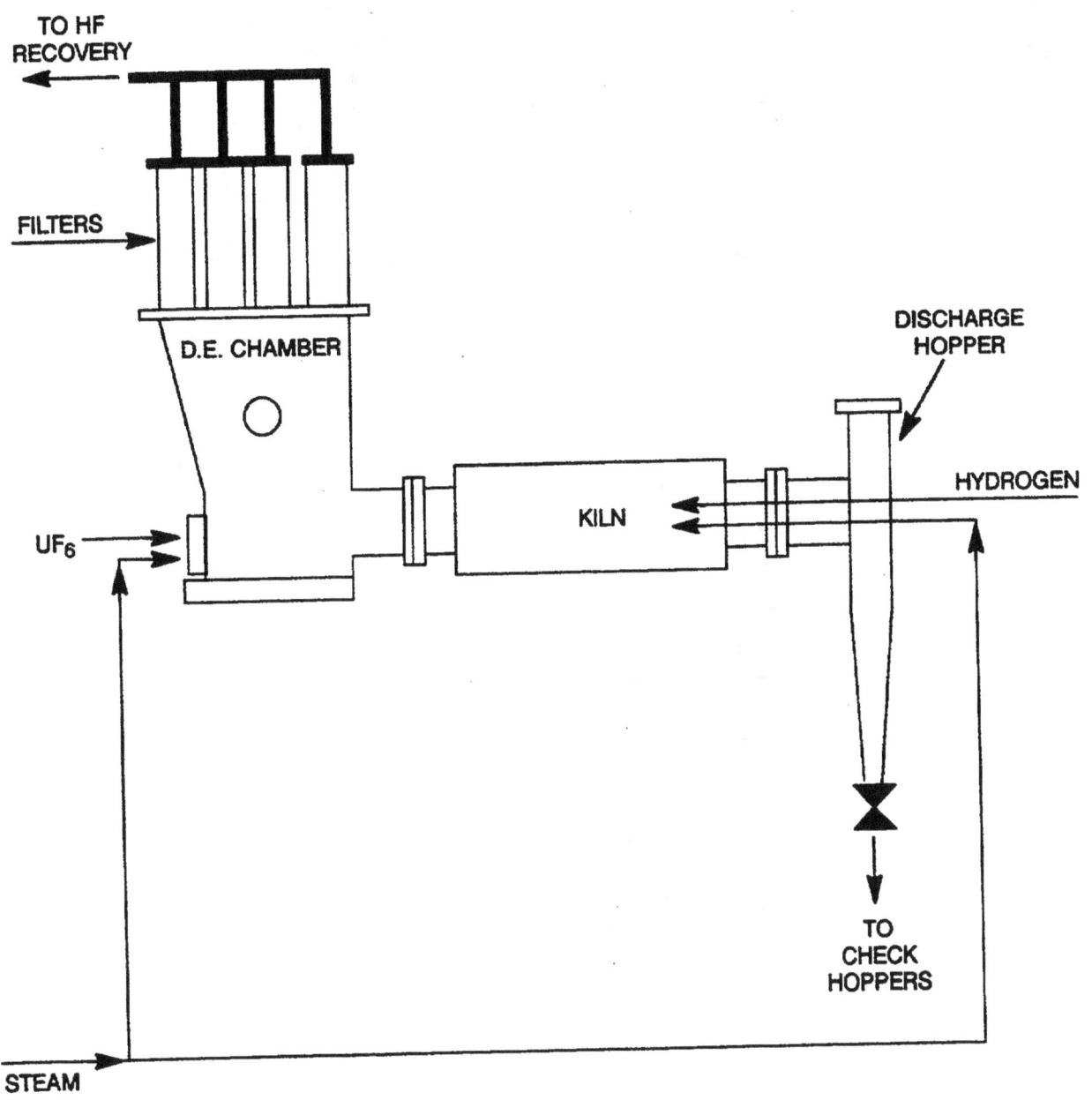

Figure B.3

UF$_6$ Dry Conversion Process
Hydrolysis Operation

B-7

Table B-1 HAZOP Study Table

Item Number	Deviation	Causes	Consequences	Safeguards
		5.0 VESSEL - VAPORIZER STEAM CHEST		
5.1	High Level	Level probe failure	Potential criticality concern - Loss of barrier	Vaporizer gravity drain
		Normal condensate drain overwhelmed or plugged and passive overflow line plugged	Potential safety concern - Cylinder floating, breaking pigtail	Passive overflow line with strainer to prevent line plugging
		High flow in the emergency cooling water line (Item 4.1)		Preventive maintenance on vaporizer.
				Administrative control to check for debris (foreign material) after maintenance and before each cylinder installation
				* (Note: During the Nuclear Criticality Safety Evaluation (NCSE), it was determined that this interlock cannot be regarded as a criticality safety significant interlock for slab thickness.)
				Operability test of level float at each cylinder installation
				High-level alarm

B-8

Table B-1 (Cont'd)

5.0 VESSEL - VAPORIZER STEAM CHEST (Continued)

Item Number	Deviation	Causes	Consequences	Safeguards
5.2	Low level		No consequence of interest (NCI)	
5.3	High temperature	High flow in the 120-psig plant steam to vaporizer (raw steam) (Item 2.1)	Potential loss of containment if the temperature exceeds the temperature rating of the cylinder vessel (Item 5.11)	High-temperature alarm Temperature indication
		Low/no flow in the emergency cooling water line when needed (Item 4.2)		
5.4	Low temperature	Low/no flow in the 120-psig plant steam line to the vaporizer (Item 2.2)	Potential loss of production form solid UF$_6$ plug in the pigtail; also unable to maintain the cylinder pressure	Temperature indication
5.5	High pressure in the vaporizer steam chest	Valve in vent line closed	Release of steam with the potential for injury to personnel (e.g., burn hazard)	Conservation vent valve on vaporizer vent line (relieves at 2 inches (WC) pressure)
		High pressure in the steam supply (Item 2.7)		
		Low/no flow in the vaporizer steam chest vent line to scrubbers S-675 (A&B) (Item 6.2)	Potential leak (Item 5.11) Potential rupture (Item 5.12)	
5.6	Low pressure in the vaporizer steam chest	Rapid cooling of the steam chest or steam condensation	Potential process upset	Conservation vent valve on vaporizer vent line (draws air in at 1-inch WC vacuum)

B-9

Table B-1 (Cont'd)

Item Number	Deviation	Causes	Consequences	Safeguards
		5.0 VESSEL - VAPORIZER STEAM CHEST (Continued)		
5.7	High pressure in the UF$_6$ cylinder	Low/no flow in the emergency cooling water (Item 4.2)	Potential criticality concern (UO$_2$F$_2$-H$_2$O in the vaporizer)- Damage pigtail and release UF$_6$ to the vaporizer and the atmosphere	High-pressure indication and alarm in UF$_6$ gas line to the kiln
		Heat overfilled cylinder	High flow in the UF$_6$ gas line to the kiln (Item 7.1)	Administrative controls to verify net weight of cylinder is less than maximum safe fill limits before use
5.8	Low pressure in the UF$_6$ cylinder	Empty UF$_6$ cylinder	Potential criticality concern - Backflow of moderator into UF$_6$ cylinder (Item 7.3)	
			Low pressure in the UF$_6$ gas line to the kiln (Item 7.8)	
5.9	High concentration of dirt, dust, rust, and debris	High concentration of rust in the emergency cooling water (Item 4.11)	NCI - Conductivity false alarm	Conductivity monitor
		Accumulation of dirt, dust, and debris during maintenance	Potential for plugging drain lines	Administrative control to check for debris (foreign material) after maintenance and before each cylinder installation
5.10	High concentration of UF$_6$	UF$_6$ cylinder leak or rupture	Potential release or personnel exposure to UF$_6$ and/or HF acid	Ventilation scrubber to remove potential UF$_6$ or HF releases and prevent release to the atmosphere
		Reverse flow in the vaporizer steam chest vent line to scrubbers S-675 (A&B) (Item 6.3)	Potential criticality concern	Detect breach of UF$_6$ containment in vaporizer
		Low temperature in the vaporizer steam chest, valve hot box, vaporizer safe sump and check hopper vents to S-675 and S-665 A&B (Item 6.6)		Conductivity monitor

Table B-1 (Cont'd)

Item Number	Deviation	Causes	Consequences	Safeguards
		5.0 VESSEL - VAPORIZER STEAM CHEST (Continued)		
5.11	Leak of UF_6 cylinder in vaporizer steam chest	High temperature (Item 5.3)	Potential criticality concern	Administrative controls for checking for leaks
		Faulty connections on the cylinder valve	Potential release or personnel exposure to UF_6 and/or HF acid	Startup checklist
		High pressure (Item 5.5)		
		Cylinder valve leaking		
		Corrosion		Conductivity monitor
		External impact		Ventilation scrubber to remove potential UF_6 or HF releases and prevent release to the atmosphere
		Valve or gasket failure		
		Improper maintenance		
5.12	Rupture of UF_6 cylinder in vaporizer steam chest	Faulty connections on the cylinder	Potential criticality concern	Cylinder recertification every 5 years
		Cylinder valve leaking	Potential release or personnel exposure to UF_6 or HF acid	
		Crane failure		
		Pigtail failure		Ventilation scrubber to remove potential UF_6 or HF releases and prevent release to the atmosphere
		Cylinder failure		
		High pressure (Item 5.5)		
		Corrosion		Administrative controls to verify net weight of cylinder is less than maximum safe fill limits before use
		External impact		

B-11

B.3 Qualitative Fault-tree Analysis of Major UF$_6$ Release

1. INTRODUCTION

In this example, Fault Tree Analysis is used to model the scenarios leading to a uranium hexafluoride (UF$_6$) release during vaporization.

Figure B.2 shows an example system for vaporization of UF$_6$. The system consists of a vaporizer chest with steam supply, emergency cooling water, receiving tank, safe sumps, and reservoir and scrubber system. The Fault Tree for Release of UF$_6$ during Vaporization (Figure B.4 and Table B-2) is a qualitative model of the vaporizer chest only. The UF$_6$ is transported in large steel cylinders. The vaporizer chest is designed to enclose this cylinder and all its connections, and the steam condensate line is supplied with a conductivity cell (with alarm, automatic steam shutoff, and isolation capability) for the detection of leaks.

2. ANALYSIS

The first step in the analysis is to define the problem by documenting the Top Event, Existing Conditions, and Physical Boundaries. The vaporization process is studied and a logic diagram is constructed that documents all the various mechanisms that can lead to a release of UF$_6$, which is the Top Event for this tree. The logic uses AND gates to represent events that must exist simultaneously to result in the Top Event. For example, under Gate 2 in the tree, for a liquid release to the building to occur, there must be two events; a release within the chest, and a failure to detect and stop it in time (Gates 6 AND 8). The logic uses OR gates for events where any single one event can result in the Top Event. For example, under Gate 8 in the tree, there are three separate ways (failures for the steam condensate to carry UF$_6$ out; instrument fails to detect, fails to shutoff, or fails to alarm; and operator does not catch this failure.

3. EVALUATION

The next step in the analysis is to determine the minimal cutsets, shown in Table B-3 labeled as such. Since no values were assigned to this example, the computer program assigned a probability of 1 to all basic events. Qualitatively, it can be seen that a release of UF$_6$ to the buildings can occur as a result of a single event, such as an impact to the piping or valve assuming that the HEPA filters fail to contain the release. It should be noted that some events described in this tree are a combination of events (i.e., cylinder rupture is a result of an overweight cylinder and failure to check weight on arrival). Quantification of the top event would require failure rates, human error probabilities, and historical operating data.

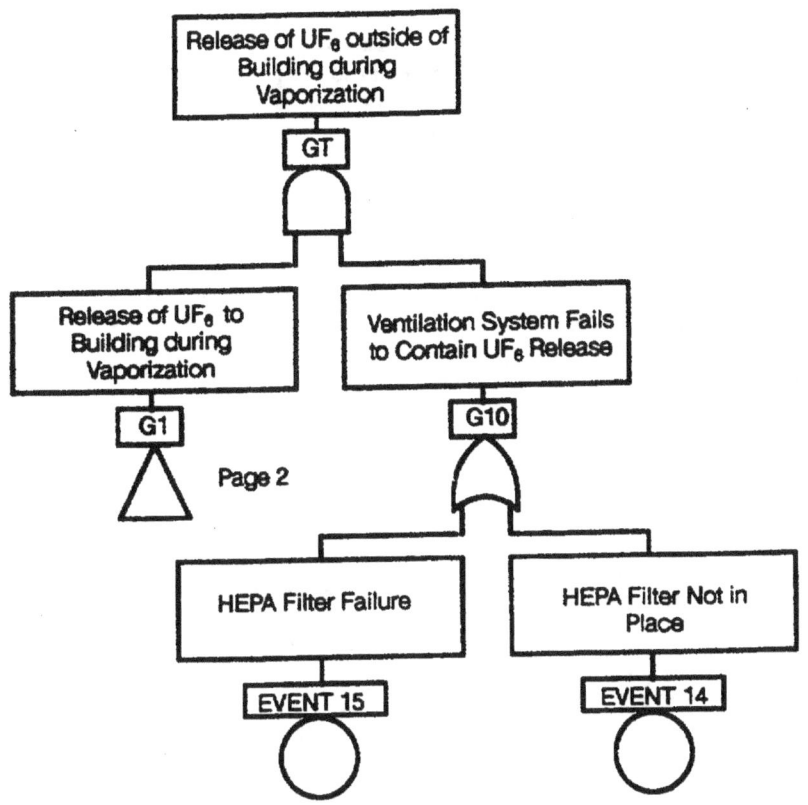

Figure B.4

Fault Tree for Release of UF$_6$ During Vaporization

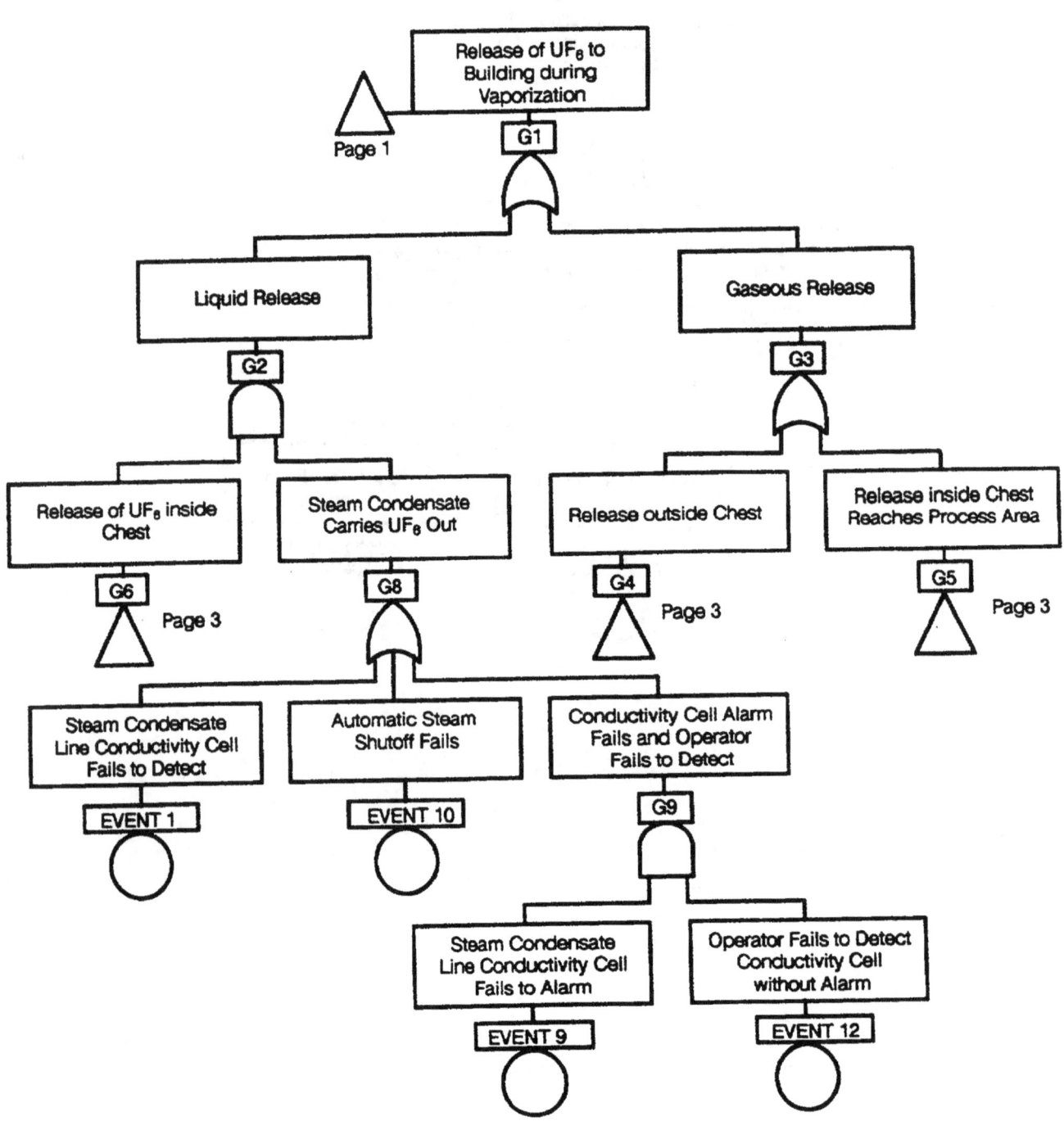

Fault Tree for Release of UF$_6$ During Vaporization (Cont.)

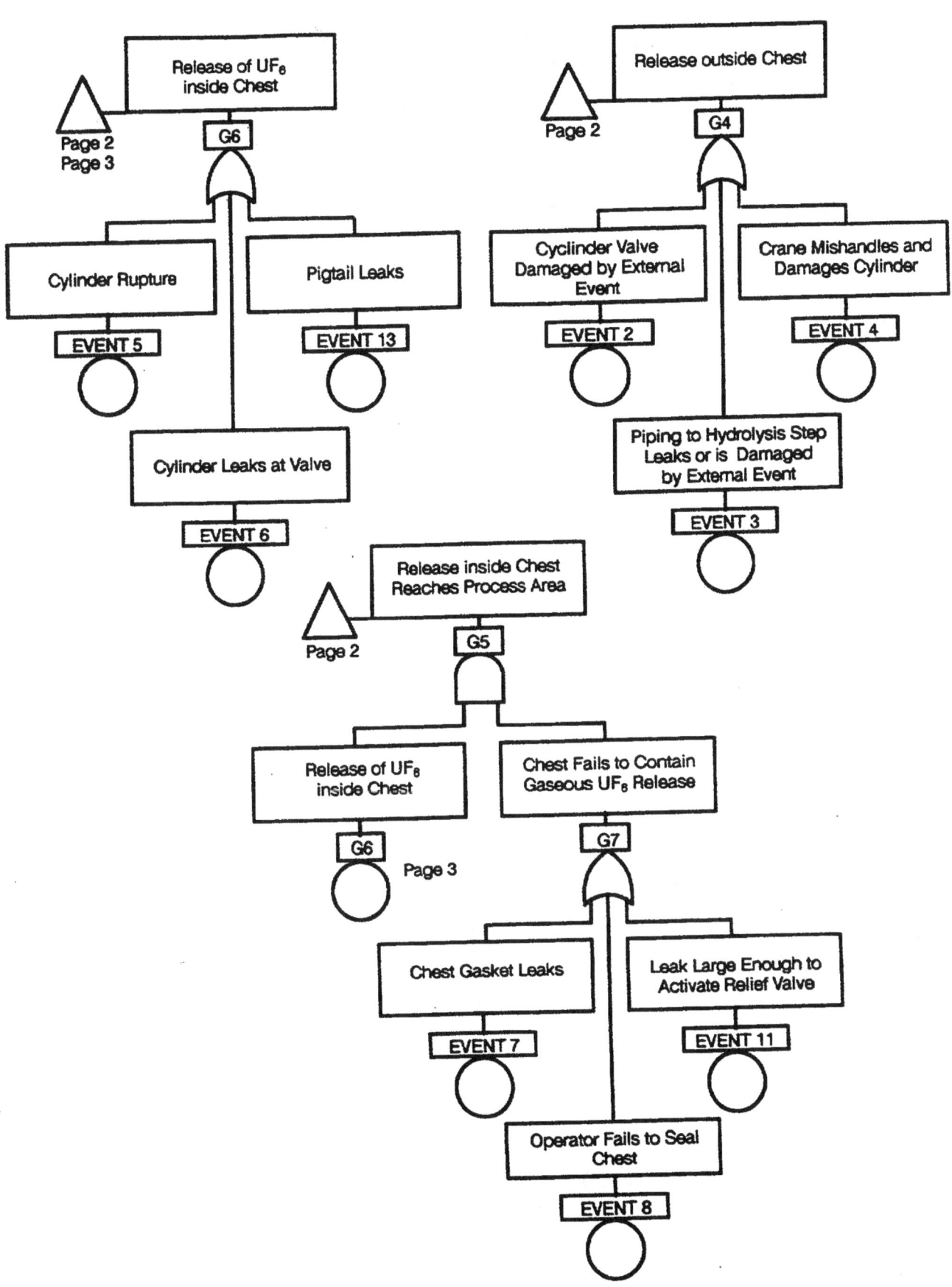

Fault Tree for Release of UF$_6$ During Vaporization (Cont.)

Table B-2
Fault Tree Event Index

Gate/Event Name	Page	Zone
EVENT1	2	1
EVENT10	2	2
EVENT11	3	7
EVENT12	2	3
EVENT13	3	2
EVENT14	1	3
EVENT15	1	2
EVENT2	3	3
EVENT3	3	4
EVENT4	3	4
EVENT5	3	1
EVENT6	3	2
EVENT7	3	6
EVENT8	3	6
EVENT9	2	2
G1	1	1
G1	2	2
G10	1	2
G2	2	2
G3	2	4
G4	2	3
G4	3	4
G5	2	4
G5	3	6
G6	2	1
G6	3	5
G7	3	6
G8	2	2
G9	2	3
GT	1	2

TABLE B-3 CUTSETS FOR EXAMPLE UF6 RELEASE FAULT TREE

Set No.	Event Name	Description	C	B.E. Prob	Calc. Result	Cutset Prob
	GT					0.00E+00
1.	EVENT11	Leak Large Enough to Activate Relief Valve				1.00E+00
	EVENT13	Pigtail Leaks.				
	EVENT15	HEPA Filter Failure				
2.	EVENT11	Leak Large Enough to Activate Relief Valve				1.00E+00
	EVENT15	HEPA Filter Failure				
	EVENT6	Cylinder Leaks at Valve.				
3.	EVENT15	HEPA Filter Failure				1.00E+00
	EVENT2	Cylinder Valve Damaged by External Event				
4.	EVENT15	HEPA Filter Failure				1.00E+00
	EVENT4	Crane Mishandles and Damages Cylinder.				
5.	EVENT15	HEPA Filter Failure				1.00E+00
	EVENT3	Piping to Hydrolysis Step Leaks or Is Damaged by External Event				
6.	EVENT11	Leak Large Enough to Activate Relief Valve				1.00E+00
	EVENT15	HEPA Filter Fail ire				
	EVENT5	Cylinder Rupture				
7.	EVENT13	Pigtail Leaks.				1.00E+00
	EVENT15	HEPA Filter Failure				
	EVENT7	Chest Gasket Leaks.				

Set No.	Event Name	Description	C	B.E. Prob	Calc. Result	Cutset Prob
8.	EVENT15	HEPA Filter Failure				1.00E+00
	EVENT6	Cylinder Leaks at Valve.				
	EVENT7	Chest Gasket Leaks.				
9.	EVENT15	HEPA Filter Failure				1.00E+00
	EVENT5	Cylinder Rupture				
	EVENT8	Operator Fails to Seal Chest.				
10.	EVENT13	Pigtail Leaks.				1.00E+00
	EVENT15	HEPA Filter Failure				
	EVENT8	Operator Fails to Seal Chest.				
11.	EVENT15	HEPA Filter Failure				1.00E+00
	EVENT6	Cylinder Leaks at Valve.				
	EVENT8	Operator Fails to Seal Chest.				
12.	EVENT12	Operator Fails to Detect Conductivity Cell without Alarm.				1.00E+00
	EVENT15	HEPA Filter Failure				
	EVENT6	Cylinder Leaks at Valve.				
	EVENT9	Steam Condensate Line Conductivity Cell Fails to Alarm				
13.	EVENT12	Operator Fails to Detect Conductivity Cell without Alarm.				1.00E+00
	EVENT15	HEPA Filter Failure				
	EVENT5	Cylinder Rupture				
	EVENT9	Steam Condensate Line Conductivity Cell Fails to Alarm				

Set No.	Event Name	Description	C	B.E. Prob	Calc. Result	Cutset Prob
14.	EVENT12	Operator Fails to Detect Conductivity Cell without Alarm.				1.00E+00
	EVENT13	Pigtail Leaks.				
	EVENT15	HEPA Filter Failure				
	EVENT9	Steam Condensate Line Conductivity Cell Fails to Alarm				
15.	EVENT14	HEPA Filter Not in Place				1.00E+00
	EVENT6	Cylinder Leaks at Valve.				
	EVENT7	Chest Gasket Leaks.				
16.	EVENT15	HEPA Filter Failure				1.00E+00
	EVENT5	Cylinder Rupture				
	EVENT7	Chest Gasket Leaks.				
17.	EVENT10	Automatic Steam Shutoff Fails.				1.00E+00
	EVENT13	Pigtail Leaks.				
	EVENT15	HEPA Filter Failure				
18.	EVENT1	Steam Condensate Line Conductivity Cell Fails to Detect.				1.00E+00
	EVENT15	HEPA Filter Failure				
	EVENT6	Cylinder Leaks at Valve.				
19.	EVENT1	Steam Condensate Line Conductivity Cell Fails to Detect.				1.00E+00
	EVENT15	HEPA Filter Failure				
	EVENT5	Cylinder Rupture				
20.	EVENT1	Steam Condensate Line Conductivity Cell Fails to Detect.				1.00E+00
	EVENT13	Pigtail Leaks.				
	EVENT15	HEPA Filter Failure				

Set No.	Event Name	Description	C	B.E. Prob	Calc. Result	Cutset Prob
21.	EVENT10	Automatic Steam Shutoff Fails.				1.00E+00
	EVENT15	HEPA Filter Failure				
	EVENT6	Cylinder Leaks at Valve.				
22.	EVENT10	Automatic Steam Shutoff Fails.				1.00E+00
	EVENT15	HEPA Filter Failure				
	EVENT5	Cylinder Rupture				
23.	EVENT11	Leak Large Enough to Activate Relief Valve				1.00E+00
	EVENT13	Pigtail Leaks.				
	EVENT14	HEPA Filter Not in Place				
24.	EVENT11	Leak Large Enough to Activate Relief Valve				1.00E+00
	EVENT14	HEPA Filter Not in Place				
	EVENT6	Cylinder Leaks at Valve.				
25.	EVENT14	HEPA Filter Not in Place				1.00E+00
	EVENT2	Cylinder Valve Damaged by External Event				
26.	EVENT14	HEPA Filter Not in Place				1.00E+00
	EVENT4	Crane Mishandles and Damages Cylinder.				
27.	EVENT14	HEPA Filter Not in Place				1.00E+00
	EVENT3	Piping to Hydrolysis Step Leaks or Is Damaged by External Event.				
28.	EVENT14	HEPA Filter Not in Place				1.00E+00
	EVENT5	Cylinder Rupture				
	EVENT8	Operator Fails to Seal Chest.				

Set No.	Event Name	Description	C	B.E. Prob	Calc. Result	Cutset Prob
29.	EVENT13	Pigtail Leaks.				1.00E+00
	EVENT14	HEPA Filter Not in Place				
	EVENT7	Chest Gasket Leaks.				
30.	EVENT14	HEPA Filter Not in Place				1.00E+00
	EVENT6	Cylinder Leaks at Valve.				
	EVENT8	Operator Fails to Seal Chest.				

B.4 Interaction Matrix for ADU Process

Table B-4 Chemical Matrix for ADU Process

	UF_6	UNH	UO_2F_2	ADU	HF	HNO_3	NH_4OH	NH_3	H_2O	STEAM	N_2
UF_6		X				X			X	X	
UNH	X										
UO_2F_2											
ADU											
HF							X	X			
HNO_3	X						X	X			
NH_4OH					X	X					
NH_3					X	X					
H_2O	X										
STEAM	X										
N_2											

X - Indicates incompatability, potential worker hazard.

Table B-5 Reactive Chemical Hazards for ADU Process

No	Chemical Name	Hazard Information	Bretherick 3rd e
			Reference page
1	Ammonia	Potentially violent or explosive reactor contact with nitric acid. A jet of ammonia will ignite in nitric acid vapor (ambient temperature). Incompatable with HF, HNO_3, and UF_6. Emits toxic fumes of NO_2 when heated.	1177
2	Ammonium Hydroxide	Incompatable with HF, HNO_3, and UF_6	1205
3	Hydrogen Fluoride	Violent reaction with NH_4OH Reacts with steam or water to produce toxic and corrosive fumes.	1044
4	Nitric Acid	The common chemical most frequently involved in reactive incidents; reactions do not generally require addition of heat. Ignition on contact with HF. Incompatible with NH_4OH Will react with steam or water to produce heat and toxic and corrosive fumes. The oxidizing power and hazard potential of HNO_3 increase with concentration.	1100
5	Uranium Hexafluoride	Violent reaction with water	1078
6	Uranyl Nitrate (UNH)	Decomposes at 100 °C	1302
7	Steam		
8	Water		

Notes: 1. MP at 2 atmospheres. Volatile crystals sublime. Triple point - 64.0 °C.

Chemical reactions:

1. $UF_6 + UO_2(NO_3)_2.6H_2O + water \longrightarrow UO_2F_2 + 4HF + UO_2(NO_3)_2.6H_2O + heat$

   or, in the absence of water, UF_6 could strip some water from UNH, for example,
   $3UF_6 + 2UO_2(NO_3)_2.6H_2O \longrightarrow 3UO_2F_2 + 6HF + UO_2(NO_3)_2.3H_2O$
   (Other similar reactions are also possible.)

2. $UF_6 + HNO_3 + water \longrightarrow UO_2F_2 + 4HF + HNO_3 + heat$

3. $UF_6 + 2H_2O \longrightarrow UO_2F_2 + 4HF$

4. $UF_6 + Steam \longrightarrow UO_2F_2 + 4HF$

5. $HF + NH_4OH \longrightarrow NH_4F + H_2O$

6. $HF + NH_4OH \longrightarrow NH_4F + H_2O$

7. $HNO_3 + NH_4OH \longrightarrow NH_4NO_3 + H_2O$

8. $HNO_3 + NH_3 \longrightarrow NH_4NO_3$

None of the above reactions requires elevated temperatures or pressures.

Ammonium fluoride (CAS No. 12125-01-8) has MW = 37.1 and decomposes on heating. It is corrosive to tissue. Ammonium nitrate (CAS No. 6484-52-2) has MW = 80.1 and MP = 169.6°C and decomposes above 210°C, evolving nitrogen oxides. A powerful oxidizer, it may explode under confinement and high temperatures. Uranium oxyfluoride (CAS No. 13536-84-0) has MW = 308.0 and emits toxic F-fumes when heated to decomposition. Its regulatory limits are measured as uranium.

APPENDIX C

Subsystem Analysis and Integration

Subsystem Analysis and Integration

A systematic approach to hazards analysis is essential to ensure that completeness is accomplished. Historically, errors that occur in safety analyses are non-conservative; that is, hazards and accidents are overlooked, interactions ignored, frequencies underestimated, and consequences estimated at levels less than what might be reasonably expected. Thus, the first consideration that should be handled is systematically establishing the boundaries or limits to be analyzed. Boundaries must be established, for individual analyses, comprising the total assessment. To establish these analytical limits, we must determine if material or energy can be transferred away from an accident in a manner that can adversely affect people, equipment, processes, or the environment. The distance outward is governed by the limits established by consequences judged to be significant.

Given the outer bounds of the overall analysis, the next step is to decide on whether a single, all-encompassing analysis should be made or whether to subdivide the analysis into smaller increments. Large, single analyses are typically complex and cumbersome but enable the analyst to include all interactions that can occur among systems. Dividing the overall analysis into small independent studies reduces the complexity; however, it increases the possibility of omitting system interactions and common-cause effects or failures. The pragmatic approach is to perform several separate analyses, but ensure that both output and input of materials and energies that can affect each analysis are properly considered. This is illustrated in Figure C.1.

In system A, the energy released by an accident does not have an impact beyond the system boundary. The materials released do not impact other systems, but do contribute to the impact on the overall analysis. System A is, therefore, a candidate for an analysis independent of the other systems to be considered.

In System B, the energy released by an accident adversely impacts System C. The materials released do not impact other systems, but do contribute to the impact on the overall analysis. The effects of the materials released from this system define the envelope of the overall analysis. Because System B is unaffected by the other systems, it, too, may be analyzed independently. However, the energy impact from System B to System C must be considered in the analysis of System C.

In system C, the energy released by an accident adversely impacts system D, and the materials released from System D adversely impact System C. Because of the interactions of the two systems, consideration should be given to analyzing both systems together to avoid omitting common-cause effects that the interactions might have.

Examples of accidents that might fall into the various categories could be an uncontrolled chemical reaction in System A, an explosion in System B that damages equipment in System C, and a fire in System C that releases flammable gases in System D that intensify the fire in System C and propagate to System D.

Each system must be analyzed separately for each accident.

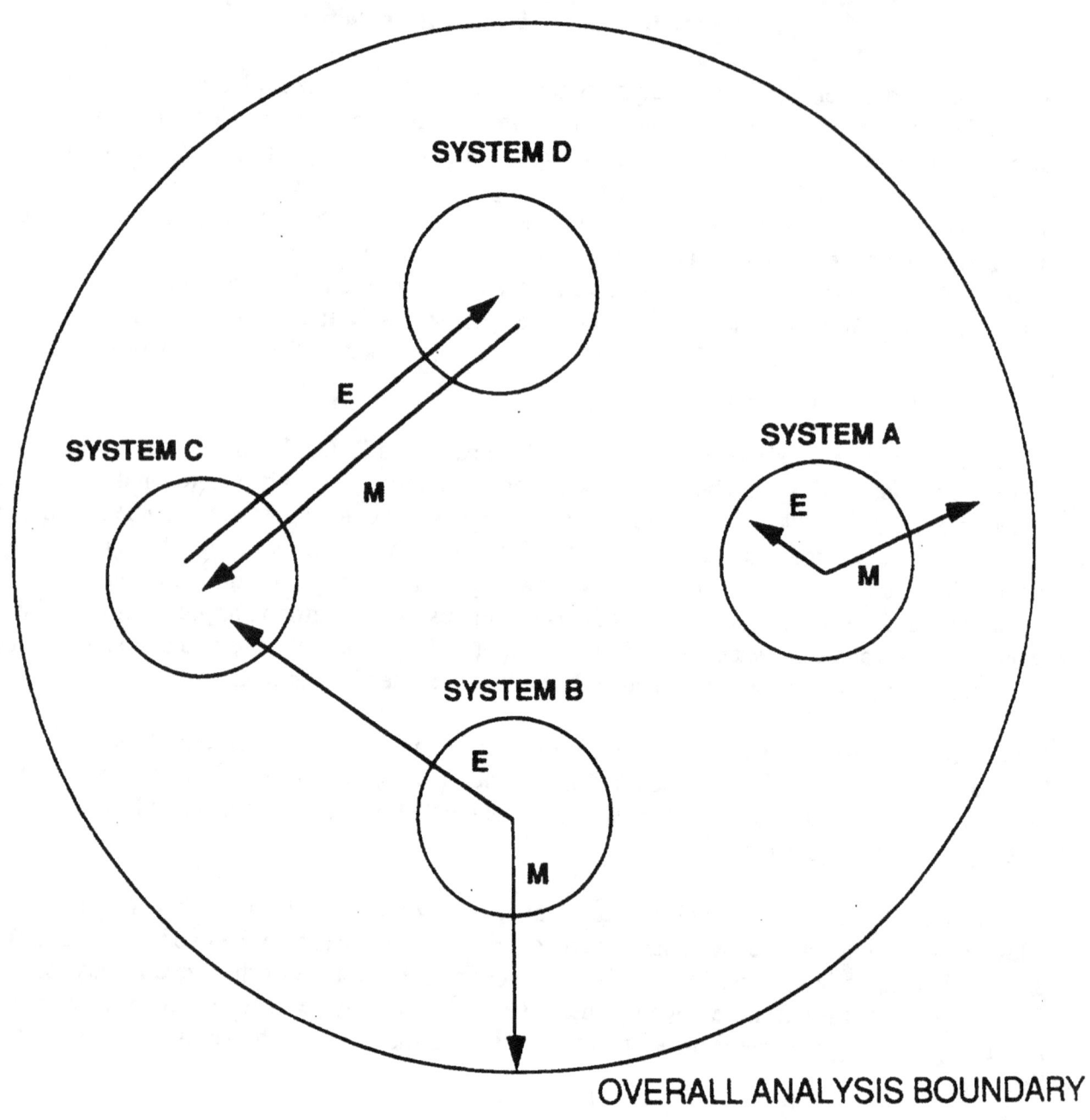

Figure C.1

Selection of overall and individual analyses.

NRC FORM 335 (2-89)	U.S. NUCLEAR REGULATORY COMMISSION	1. REPORT NUMBER (Assigned by NRC, Add Vol., Supp., Rev., and Addendum Numbers, if any.)

NRC FORM 335
(2-89)
NRCM 1102,
3201, 3202

U.S. NUCLEAR REGULATORY COMMISSION

BIBLIOGRAPHIC DATA SHEET

(See instructions on the reverse)

1. REPORT NUMBER
(Assigned by NRC, Add Vol., Supp., Rev.,
and Addendum Numbers, if any.)

NUREG 1513

2. TITLE AND SUBTITLE

Integrated Safety Analysis Guidance Document

3. DATE REPORT PUBLISHED

MONTH	YEAR
May	2001

4. FIN OR GRANT NUMBER

5. AUTHOR(S)

Richard I. Milstein

6. TYPE OF REPORT

7. PERIOD COVERED *(Inclusive Dates)*

8. PERFORMING ORGANIZATION - NAME AND ADDRESS *(If NRC, provide Division, Office or Region, U.S. Nuclear Regulatory Commission, and mailing address; if contractor, provide name and mailing address.)*

Division of Fuel Cycle Safety and Safeguards
Office of Nuclear Material Safety and Safeguards
U. S. Nuclear Regulatory Commission
Washington, D. C. 20555-0001

9. SPONSORING ORGANIZATION - NAME AND ADDRESS *(If NRC, type "Same as above"; if contractor, provide NRC Division, Office or Region, U.S. Nuclear Regulatory Commission, and mailing address.)*

Same as above

10. SUPPLEMENTARY NOTES

11. ABSTRACT *(200 words or less)*

On September 18, 2000, the U. S. Nuclear Regulatory Commission published a final rule, 10 CFR Part 70, for licensing the use of special nuclear material. In this rule, NRC included a requirement that certain licensee/applicants subject to 10 CFR 70 conduct an integrated safety analysis (ISA). The purpose of this document is to provide general guidance to NRC fuel cycle licensee/applicants on how to perform an integrated safety analysis (ISA) and document the results. In particular, the document defines an ISA, identifies its role in a facility's safety program, identifies and describes several generally accepted ISA methods, and provides guidance in choosing a method.

The approaches and methods described in this document are not a substitute for NRC regulations, and compliance is not required. This document does not itself impose regulatory requirements, nor does it address acceptance criteria for an ISA. As discussed in Section 1.3, "Purpose of Document," acceptance criteria for ISA are addressed in the "Standard Review Plan for the Review of a License Application for a Fuel Cycle Facility," draft NUREG-1520.

12. KEY WORDS/DESCRIPTORS *(List words or phrases that will assist researchers in locating the report.)*

integrated safety analysis
hazard analysis technique
what-if-analysis
HAZOP analysis
fault-tree analysis

13. AVAILABILITY STATEMENT

unlimited

14. SECURITY CLASSIFICATION

(This Page)

unclassified

(This Report)

unclassified

15. NUMBER OF PAGES

16. PRICE

NRC FORM 335 (2-89)

This form was electronically produced by Elite Federal Forms, Inc.

NUREG-1513

INTEGRATED SAFETY ANALYSIS GUIDANCE DOCUMENT

MAY 2001

UNITED STATES
NUCLEAR REGULATORY COMMISSION
WASHINGTON, DC 20555-0001

OFFICIAL BUSINESS
PENALTY FOR PRIVATE USE, $300

www.ingramcontent.com/pod-product-compliance
Lightning Source LLC
Chambersburg PA
CBHW081849280526
45789CB00007B/2620